AURORA PUBLIC LIBRARY

PROPERTY OF
COMMUNITY COLLEGE OF AURORA
AURORA PUBLIC LIBRARY

PR   Watts, Cedric Thomas.
6005
.04   Joseph Conrad
Z9237
1989
823.912 Wat

JOSEPH CONRAD

Literary Lives
General Editor: Richard Dutton, Senior Lecturer in English,
University of Lancaster

This series offers stimulating accounts of the literary careers of the most widely read British and Irish authors. Volumes follow the outline of writers' working lives, not in the spirit of traditional biography, but aiming to trace the professional, publishing and social contexts which shaped their writing. The role and status of 'the author' as the creator of literary texts is a vexed issue in current critical theory, where a variety of social, linguistic and psychological approaches have challenged the old concentration on writers as specially-gifted individuals. Yet reports of 'the death of the author' in literary studies are (as Mark Twain said of a premature obituary) an exaggeration. This series aims to demonstrate how an understanding of writers' careers can promote, for students and general readers alike, a more informed historical reading of their works.

Joseph Conrad

A Literary Life

Cedric Watts

Professor of English
University of Sussex

PROPERTY OF AURORA PUBLIC LIBRARY

PROPERTY OF
COMMUNITY COLLEGE OF AURORA
AURORA PUBLIC LIBRARY

St. Martin's Press   New York

AUG   1990

© Cedric Watts 1989
All rights reserved. For information, write:
Scholarly and Reference Division,
St. Martin's Press, Inc., 175 Fifth Avenue, New York, NY 10010

First published in the United States of America in 1989

Printed and bound in Great Britain

ISBN 0–312–03089–4

Library of Congress Cataloging-in-Publication Data
Watts, Cedric Thomas.
Joseph Conrad: a literary life.
(Literary lives)
Bibliography: p.
Includes index.
1. Conrad, Joseph, 1857–1924. 2. Novelists, English—
20th century—Biography. I. Title. II. Series:
Literary lives (New York, N.Y.)
PR6005.04Z9237 1989 823'.912 [B]   88–35557
ISBN 0–312–03089–4

3 1277 00564 9865

Contents

Contents

1

Preliminary Matter

1.1 PREFACE

This book was commissioned as part of a series with a distinctive specification. I'll quote the general editor's 'Outline of Policy' to give you the main notions:

> The volumes of the series will not be works of literary criticism but attempts to sketch out sufficient detail about the lives, publishing contexts and intellectual backgrounds of the authors for any reader subsequently to be able to make an informed historical reading of the authors' lives. . . . . The series will concentrate on the literary *career*, focusing on matters which have a demonstrable bearing either on what authors actually wrote or on the conditions under which they wrote. The series will thus have a practical and factual emphasis, and . . . . . issues such as patronage and subscription, or practical considerations such as writing for the theatre, or for periodical publication, would thus figure prominently, as would anything giving rise to an author's revision of his texts. . . . .
> The factual, biographical base may thus help to keep the 'intellectual milieu' element of the literary life (which is theoretically inexhaustible) within reasonable limits. Such considerations will be important in keeping to a 60,000 word target. . . . .

The opening declaration that volumes in this series 'will not be works of literary criticism' may need some qualification. Documentary material about Conrad would have little point if it could not be shown to have some bearing on the content and variable quality of Conrad's writings. Even the selection of one fact rather than another is a matter of evaluation; so 'documentary material' here is impelled by the spirit of criticism, just as (conversely) Conrad's tales, at their most exuberantly imaginative, are impelled by the desire to tell truths about the real world; and if circumstances often contorted that impulsion, the contortions can still be construed as truth-tellers. To talk of 'truth' rather than 'ideology' or 'inter-subjectivity' may be forgiven as an echo of Conrad, the courage of whose quest for veracity was proportionate to the corrosiveness of his scepticism about the quest's goal. His fiction sometimes reminds us of Nietzsche's aphorism: 'Truths are illusions of which we have forgotten that they are illusions.'

In accordance with the series-format, the plan of this book is as follows. Part 2 offers a chronological table followed by a concise biographical survey which gives particular attention to the financing of Conrad's remarkable odyssey through the world. Part 3 gives illustrations of Conrad's cultural milieu and of his ability to create a distinctive literary identity by learning from a multiplicity of exemplars. Part 4 follows his career as a writer from the early days of struggle to the late days of popular success, emphasising the material circumstances of his literary production. These pages depict the tension which Conrad experienced between the claims of artistic integrity and the demands of the market-place; they also consider the various kinds of suasion and sustenance provided by his publishers and editors, friends and collaborators. Modes of censorship form a topic of the Conclusion.

One thesis of this book is that, although Conrad gave frequent and eloquent expression to the wretchedness of his plight as an author, he was remarkably fortunate in his circumstances, given not only the amount of sympathetic support and financial aid that he received but also the size and diversity of the market for his work. A second thesis is that consequently his output is much larger than it may at first appear, since a single work might be published in a variety of forms. *The Nigger of the 'Narcissus'*, to take just one example, changed markedly between its serial form and its initial book form, and there are further textual variations between the various editions of the book – and even small variations between different impressions of a single edition. Thirdly, we can observe that Conrad's situation as a writer for posterity who was also seeking to earn his bread and butter by his pen led him to make some painful (even unethical) compromises, and these relate thematically to his main works, which so vividly render the corruption of integrity by 'material interests'. A large general point made in the ensuing pages is that when we consider his career historically, emphasis falls less on Conrad as the author of 'canonical texts' for academic study than on Conrad as communicator – a writer who, in the burgeoning era of mass-communications, was able to address his public (on both sides of the Atlantic) through popular magazines and newspapers as well as through the pages of elegant volumes. His mood was sometimes haughtily patrician; but the very exigencies of the market importuned the solidarity of this seer with 'all the hearts that beat in the darkness'.

The co-ordinating theme of the subsequent chapters is 'indebtedness': Conrad's cultural, social and financial indebtedness to others, and our literary indebtedness to Conrad. In view of the range and variety of his career, the 60 000-word limit on this discussion is quite severe; but the consequent economics may perhaps lend this book an introductory clarity. The teacher of languages in *Under Western Eyes* declares: 'Words, as is well known, are the great foes of reality.' If he is right, the series-format at least restricts the damage.

1.2 ACKNOWLEDGEMENTS AND EDITORIAL NOTES

When preparing this book, I was particularly indebted to the following works. Andrzej Busza, 'Conrad's Polish Literary Background and Some Aspects of the Influence of Polish Literature on His Work', in *Antemurale*, vol. X (Roma: Institutum Historicum Polonicum, 1966). Zdzisław Najder, *Conrad's Polish Background: Letters to and from Polish Friends* (London: Oxford University Press, 1964) and *Joseph Conrad: A Chronicle* (Cambridge: Cambridge University Press, 1983). *The Collected Letters of Joseph Conrad*, edited by Frederick R. Karl and Laurence Davies (Cambridge: Cambridge University Press, 1983 onwards). Professor Davies kindly supplied me with proofs of Volume III, which had not yet been published when this book was written. Andrzej Busza and Hans van Marle generously provided scholarly advice. The publishers of my *Preface to Conrad* (London: Longman, 1982) kindly permitted me to adapt here some of its paragraphs. Alan Sinfield was, as usual, shrewdly encouraging. Dr G. Hemstedt kindly helped to check the proofs.

In any quotation, a row of three dots (. . .) indicates an ellipsis already present in the printed text, whereas a row of five dots indicates an omission that I have made. All other emendations to quoted passages are given in square brackets. With these exceptions, I have endeavoured to present all quoted material without correction or alteration.

In accordance with 'house style', large numbers are given with spaces instead of commas. Thus '6,153,000' is represented as '6 153 000'.

This book was written in 1986 and 1987.

2
Biographical

2.1 CHRONOLOGICAL TABLE

1857: Conrad (Józef Teodor Konrad Korzeniowski) born at Berdyczów (Ukrainian: Berdichev) in partitioned Poland.

1861: Conrad's father, Apollo Korzeniowski, arrested for patriotic conspiracy.

1862: Apollo and his wife, Ewa, sent into exile in northern Russia; Conrad travels with them.

1865: Conrad's mother dies of tuberculosis.

1867: Apollo Korzeniowski, suffering from tuberculosis, is permitted to reside in Galicia.

1869: Apollo Korzeniowski dies in Kraków. Tadeusz Bobrowski becomes Conrad's guardian.

1874: Conrad travels to Marseille to become a seaman.

1878: Conrad attempts suicide, recovers, and later enters British Merchant Navy.

1880: Qualifies as second mate.

1883: Shipwrecked.

1884: Qualifies as first mate.

1886: Becomes a British subject; qualifies as master.

1887: First mate of barque *Highland Forest*.

1888: His first command: the barque *Otago*.

1889: Begins *Almayer's Folly*.

1890: The Congo journey.

1891: First mate of clipper *Torrens*; meets Galsworthy on board.

1893: Second mate of steamship *Adowa*.

1894: Bobrowski dies; Conrad inherits about £1600; *Almayer's Folly* accepted for publication by T. Fisher Unwin.

1895: *Almayer's Folly* published (London: Unwin; New York: Macmillan); reviews vary but include high praise.

1896: *An Outcast of the Islands* published (London: Unwin; New York: Appleton; Leipzig: Tauchnitz). Conrad marries Jessie George. 'The Idiots' published in *Savoy*.

1

1897: *The Nigger of the 'Narcissus'* serialised in Henley's *New Review* (extracts in *Country Life*, New York) and in *Illustrated Buffalo Express* (USA), and published as a book by Heinemann in London and by Dodd, Mead & Co. (under the title *The Children of the Sea*) in New York. Conrad meets Cunninghame Graham and Stephen Crane. 'The Lagoon' published in *Cornhill Magazine*, 'An Outpost of Progress' in *Cosmopolis*, and 'Karain' in *Blackwood's Magazine* and *Living Age*.

1898: Birth of son, Borys; Conrad meets Ford Madox Hueffer (later known as Ford Madox Ford) and Henry James. *Tales of Unrest* ('Karain', 'The Idiots', 'An Outpost of Progress', 'The Return', 'The Lagoon') published (London: Unwin; New York: Scribner's; Leipzig: Tauchnitz). 'Alphonse Daudet' and 'Tales of the Sea' in *Outlook* (London); 'An Observer in Malaya' in *Academy*; 'Youth' in *Blackwood's* and in *Outlook* (New York).

1899: 'Heart of Darkness' serialised in *Blackwood's*. J. B. Pinker offers to become Conrad's literary agent.

1899–1900: *Lord Jim* serialised in *Blackwood's*.

1900: *Lord Jim* published as book (Edinburgh and London: Blackwood; New York: Doubleday; Toronto: Gage). 'Heart of Darkness' serialised in *Living Age*.

1901: *The Inheritors*, with Hueffer as co-author (London: Heinemann; New York: McClure, Phillips). 'Amy Foster' in *Illustrated London News*.

1902: 'The End of the Tether' in *Blackwood's*. *Youth* volume ('Youth', 'Heart of Darkness', 'The End of the Tether') published (Edinburgh and London: Blackwood). 'Typhoon' serialised in *Pall Mall Magazine* and in *Critic* (New York); published as a book (New York and London: Putnam). 'Tomorrow' in *Pall Mall Magazine*. Preface to *The Nigger* issued as booklet.

1903: *Youth* volume published in New York (McClure, Phillips). *Typhoon and Other Stories* ('Typhoon', 'Amy Foster', 'Falk', 'Tomorrow') published (London: Heinemann). *Romance*, a collaboration with Hueffer, published (London: Smith, Elder & Co.). *'Falk', 'Amy Foster', 'To-morrow': Three Stories* (New York: McClure, Phillips).

1904: Jessie Conrad injures her knees and is partially disabled for life. *Romance* (New York: McClure, Phillips). *Nostromo* serialised in *T. P.'s Weekly* and published as book (London and New York: Harper). 'Missing', 'Overdue' and 'Stranded' (subsequently entitled 'Overdue and Missing' and 'The Grip of the Land') in *Daily Mail*; 'Anatole France [*Crainquebille*]' in *Speaker*; 'London River' (subsequently 'The Faithful River') in *World Today* and *World's Work*; 'On the North Sea Outrage' in *The Times*.

1905: *One Day More* (dramatisation of 'Tomorrow') unsuccessfully staged. 'Henry James' in *North American Review*, 'Landfalls and Departures', 'Up Anchor' (subsequently 'Emblems of Hope') and 'Gales of Wind' (subsequently 'The Character of the Foe') in *Pall Mall Magazine* and *Reader Magazine*; 'The Fine Art' in *Pall Mall Magazine*; 'The Tallness of the Spars' (subsequently 'Cobwebs and Gossamer') and 'The Weight of the Burden' in *Harper's Weekly*; 'Autocracy and War' in *Fortnightly Review* and *North American Review*; 'Books' in *Speaker* and *Living Age*; 'Her Captivity' (later 'In Captivity') in *Blackwood's*; 'The Heroic Age' in *Standard*; 'The Art of Fiction' (preface to *The Nigger*) in *Harper's Weekly*; 'London River' in *Metropolitan Magazine*.

1906: Second son (John) born. *The Mirror of the Sea* published (London: Methuen; New York: Harper; Leipzig: Tauchnitz). 'Initiation' in *Blackwood's*; 'A Middle-Class Family' (later 'John Galsworthy') in *Outlook*; 'Gaspar Ruiz' in *Pall Mall Magazine* and *Saturday Evening Post*; 'An Anarchist' and 'The Informer' in *Harper's Magazine*; 'The Brute' in *Daily Chronicle*; 'My Best Story' and 'An Outpost of Progress' in *Grand Magazine*; 'The "Tremolino" ' in *Tribune*.

1906–7: *The Secret Agent* serialised in *Ridgway's*.

1907: *The Secret Agent*: book (London: Methuen; New York: Harper; Leipzig: Tauchnitz). 'The Brute' in *McClure's Magazine*; 'Rulers of East and West' in *Reader Magazine*; 'The Censor of Plays' in *Daily Mail*.

1908: 'The Duel' in *Pall Mall Magazine* and (under title 'The Point of Honor') in *Forum* and as book (New York: McClure); 'The Black Mate' in *London Magazine*; 'Il Conde' in *Cassell's Magazine*; 'Anatole France [*L'Ile des pingouins*]' in *English Review*. *A Set of Six* ('Gaspar Ruiz', 'The Informer', 'The Brute', 'An Anarchist', 'The Duel', 'Il Conde'): London: Methuen; Leipzig: Tauchnitz. 'Rulers of East and West' in *Putnam's Magazine*.

1908–9: *Some Reminiscences* (later entitled *A Personal Record*) serialised in Hueffer's *English Review*.

1909: 'The Nature of a Crime' (co-authored with Hueffer) in *English Review*. 'Il Conde' in *Harper's Magazine*; 'The Silence of the Sea' in *Daily Mail*.

1910: Conrad has breakdown after completing *Under Western Eyes*. 'The Secret Sharer' in *Harper's Magazine*; 'The Life Beyond', 'A Happy Wanderer' and 'The Ascending Effort' in *Daily Mail*.

1910–11: *Under Western Eyes* serialised in *English Review* and *North American Review*.

1911: *Under Western Eyes*, book (London: Methuen; New York: Harper; Leipzig: Tauchnitz). 'A Smile of Fortune' in *London Magazine*; 'Prince Roman' in *Oxford and Cambridge Review*; 'The Partner' in *Harper's Magazine*.

1912: *Some Reminiscences*: London: Nash; and (under the title *A Personal Record*) New York: Harper. 'Freya of the Seven Isles' in *Metropolitan Magazine* and *London Magazine*. *'Twixt Land and Sea* ('A Smile of Fortune', 'The Secret Sharer', 'Freya of the Seven Isles'): London: Dent; New York: Doran; Leipzig: Tauchnitz. *Chance* serialised in *New York Herald*. 'Prince Roman' in *Metropolitan Magazine*; 'Some Reflections on the Loss of the *Titanic*' and 'Certain Aspects of the Admirable Inquiry' in *English Review*; 'The Future of Constantinople' in *The Times*; 'A Friendly Place' in *Daily Mail*.

1913: 'One Day More' in *English Review*; 'The Inn of the Two Witches' in *Pall Mall Magazine* and *Metropolitan Magazine* (New York).

1914: Book of *Chance* published in January (London: Methuen; New York: Doubleday, Page): exceptionally good sales; Conrad becomes a highly profitable author. Conrad re-visits Poland. 'The Lesson of the Collision' (subsequently 'Protection of Ocean Liners') in *Illustrated London News*; 'The Planter of Malata' and 'Because of the Dollars' in *Metropolitan Magazine*. Introduction to Maupassant's *Yvette and Other Stories*, translated by Ada Galsworthy.

1915: *A Set of Six* (New York: Doubleday, Page). *Within the Tides* ('The Planter of Malata', 'The Partner', 'The Inn of the Two Witches'): London: Dent. *Victory* appears in both *Munsey's Magazine* (New York) and *Star*, and as a book (New York:

Doubleday, Page; London: Methuen). 'Poland Revisited'
serialised in *Daily News* (under the titles 'The Shock of War',
'To Poland in War-Time', 'The North Sea on the Eve of
War' and 'My Return to Cracow') and in *Boston Evening
Transcript*. *Wisdom and Beauty from Conrad*, edited by H.
Capes (London: Melrose).

1916: *Within the Tides* (New York: Doubleday, Page). 'Poland
Revisited' in *The Book of the Homeless*. *The Shadow-Line*
serialised in *Metropolitan Magazine*.

1916–17: *The Shadow-Line* serialised in *The English Review*.

1917: Book of *The Shadow-Line* (London and Toronto: Dent; New
York: Doubleday, Page). Conrad begins to write 'Author's
Notes' for a collected edition of his works. Introduction to
Edward Garnett's *Turgenev: A Study*. 'Never Any More'
(subsequently 'Flight') in *Fledgling*; 'The Tale' in *Strand
Magazine*; 'The Warrior's Soul' in *Land and Water*.

1918: 'Tradition' in *Daily Mail*; 'Well Done!' in *Daily Chronicle*;
'First News' in *Réveille*.

1918–20: *The Arrow of Gold* serialised in *Lloyd's Magazine*.

1919: Book of *The Arrow of Gold* (New York: Doubleday, Page;
London: Unwin). 'The Tale' as booklet (London: privately
printed). *The Rescue* serialised in *Land and Water*. 'The Crime
of Partition' in *Fortnightly Review* and *Collier's Weekly*;
'Confidence' in *Daily Mail*; 'Stephen Crane: A Note without
Dates' in *London Mercury*. Introduction to Maupassant's
Mademoiselle Fifi (reprint of introduction to *Yvette*). 'Anatole
France [*Crainquebille*]' reprinted as booklet.

1919–20: *The Rescue* serialised in *Romance* (New York).

1920: *The Secret Agent* (play) written; 'Because of the Dollars'
adapted as a play, *Laughing Anne*. *The Rescue* published as
book, twenty-four years after commencement (New York:
Doubleday, Page; London and Toronto: Dent). 'Stephen
Crane: A Note without Dates' in *Bookman* (New York).
Author's note to 'Gaspar Ruiz' in *'Youth' and 'Gaspar Ruiz'*
(London: Dent). Pro-Polish cablegram in *Outlook*. 'Alphonse
Daudet' and 'Anatole France [*L'Ile des Pingouins*]' reprinted
as booklets.

1920–28: Collected editions by Doubleday (New York), Heinemann (London), Gresham (London) and Grant (Edinburgh).

1921: *Notes on My Books* (New York: Doubleday, Page; London:

Heinemann). *Notes on Life and Letters* (London and Toronto: Dent; New York: Doubleday, Page). Play of *The Secret Agent* privately printed. Conrad translates (as *The Book of Job*) Bruno Winawer's *Księga Hioba*. 'Heroes of the Straits' (subsequently 'The Dover Patrol') in *The Times*; 'The Loss of the *Dalgonar*' in *London Mercury*; 'The First Thing I Remember' in *John O'London's Weekly*. Introduction to *A Hugh Walpole Anthology*.

1922: Death of J. B. Pinker. Stage-production of *The Secret Agent* fails. 'Cookery' in *Delineator*; 'Notices to Mariners' (subsequently 'Outside Literature') in *Manchester Guardian Literary Supplement*. Foreword to J. Sutherland's *At Sea with Joseph Conrad*.

1923: Conrad gives read·ngs in United States. *The Secret Agent* (play) published (London: Laurie). *The Rover* serialised in *Pictorial Review* and published as book (New York: Doubleday, Page; London: Unwin). *Laughing Anne* (play) published (London: Morland). Preface to R. Curle's *Into the East*. Preface to Jessie Conrad's *A Handbook of Cookery*. Introduction to T. Beer's *Stephen Crane* (New York: Knopf). Foreword to A. Dawson's *Britain's Life-Boats*. 'My Hotel in Mid-Atlantic' (subsequently 'Ocean Travel') in *Evening News*; 'A Clipper Ship I Knew' (subsequently 'The *Torrens*: A Personal Tribute') in *Blue Peter* and *Collier's Weekly*; 'Outside Literature' in *Bookman* (New York); 'Christmas Day at Sea' in *Daily Mail* and *Delineator*. 'Proust as Creator' in *Marcel Proust*, edited by C. Scott-Moncrieff.

1923–7: Collected ('Uniform') edition by Dent.

1924: May: Conrad declines offer of knighthood. 3 August: Conrad dies after a heart attack; subsequently buried at Canterbury. 'The Nature of a Crime' (co-author, Hueffer) published as book (London: Duckworth; New York: Doubleday, Page). *'Laughing Anne' and 'One Day More'* (London: Castle). *Shorter Tales of Conrad* (New York: Doubleday, Page). 'Geography and Some Explorers' in *Countries of the World* and *National Geographic Magazine*; 'Legends' in *Daily Mail*.

1925: *Tales of Hearsay* ('The Warrior's Soul', 'Prince Roman', 'The Tale', 'The Black Mate') published (London: Unwin; New York: Doubleday, Page; Leipzig: Tauchnitz). *'Laughing Anne' and 'One Day More'* (New York: Doubleday, Page). The unfinished *Suspense* serialised in *Saturday Review of Literature* and published as a book (New York: Doubleday, Page; London and Toronto: Dent; Leipzig: Tauchnitz). Preface to reprint of Stephen Crane's *The Red Badge of Courage*. Collected edition by Doubleday (the 'Memorial' edition). 'The Unlighted Coast' in *The Times*. 'A Glance at Two Books' in *Forum* and (as 'The Enterprise of Writing a Book') in both *T.P.'s and Cassell's Weekly* and *Living Age*.

1926: *Last Essays* (London: Dent; New York: Doubleday, Page). 'The Congo Diary' in *Blue Peter* and *Yale Review*. *Joseph Conrad's Diary* (London: privately printed).

1927: *Joseph Conrad: Life & Letters*, written and edited by G. Jean-Aubry (London: Heinemann). *The Sisters* (fragment) published as book (New York: Gaige).

2.2 THE FINANCING OF CONRAD'S CAREERS

2.2.1 'The Making of a Man'

Joseph Conrad pursued two careers: first, that of a seaman and officer in the merchant navy; second, that of a professional fiction-writer. His progress through the first career and his entry into the second were facilitated by money provided by his uncle, Tadeusz Bobrowski; and that money derived, in turn, from the efforts of many Polish tenant farmers, mill workers and labourers: workers who probably lived and died in ignorance of the illustrious achievements that their toil had helped to make possible. Conrad was to travel far from Poland, but he retained a lifelong emotional attachment to his native land; and furthermore there was a more tangible attachment – for many years the flow of credit-notes and remittances from his uncle was a nourishing umbilicus linking the voyager in distant oceans or the writer at an urban desk to the wheat and sugar-beet of Kazimierówka.

In December 1857, Conrad – then Józef Teodor Konrad Korzeniowski – was born into a nation which had vanished from the map of Europe. By means of a series of partitions in 1772, 1792 and 1795, Poland had been annexed by Russia from the east and by Prussia and Austria from the west and south-west. The Poles were, and remain, a proudly patriotic nation, their sense of national identity being all the more intense for their lack of

national autonomy; and when a nation is annexed by hostile
powers, its preoccupation with the interlinked problems of loyalty
and treachery is intensified.

Conrad's father, Apollo Korzeniowski, was fervently patriotic;
and, as a consequence of their conspiratorial activities, both
Apollo and his wife Ewa were arrested, tried and sent into exile
by the Russian authorities; their four-year-old son accompanied
them on the melancholy journey to Vologda. So already, as a
child, Conrad would have learned that to be loyal to one principle
may entail treachery to another: service of nation may entail
subversion of a state. Partly as a result of the privations of exile,
Ewa died early of tuberculosis, in 1865; and four years later her
grieving widower joined her in death. By the age of eleven,
Conrad was an orphan, heading the vast procession of mourners
which followed his father's coffin through the streets of Kraków
in a funeral that was simultaneously a huge patriotic demonstration. Already, stamped on the boy's imagination, was an image of
the lethal cost exacted from domestic, familial life by national
political concerns; and already he knew personally the isolation
which was to be rendered with such intensity in the novels of his
mature years.

As is shown by the writings of Hobbes, Adam Smith and
Godwin (and, of course, by those of Conrad himself), one does
not have to be a Marxist in order to see that cultural matters have
their economic causes. Conrad was a junior member of a ruling
class – the *szlachta* – which had ceased to rule; the class which, in
Poland, derived its power primarily from the ownership of agricultural land. (The term 'szlachta' can be translated equally as
'nobility' and 'gentry'.) Politically, Conrad's subsequent novels
could seem paradoxical in their combination of some aristocrati-
cally conservative elements (the keen sense of honour, of tradition,
of *noblesse oblige*) and some sceptically radical elements (the hostility to capitalism and to the commercial spirit): but the paradox
dwindles when we see how strongly it relates to the values of a
traditional land-owning gentry, and particularly to a gentry which,
in the modern world, is denied its former political powers. After
the death of Apollo Korzeniowski, the rôle of Conrad's guardian
was eventually taken by Apollo's brother-in-law, Tadeusz
Bobrowski. Biographers have followed Tadeusz's lead in stressing
the temperamental conflict between Conrad's father and his uncle.
Apollo, a poet, dramatist and translator, was romantically

idealistic, impetuous, melancholy, introspective; Tadeusz, a busy land-owner, was shrewdly practical, astutely prudent, lucidly circumspect. Yet the practical uncle was also deeply patriotic, and repeatedly reminded young Conrad of the heritage and responsibilities of a Polish nobleman: in his letters he frequently addresses his ward as *'Panie Bracie'* – 'Brother-Lord' or 'Fellow-Nobleman'. When Stein in *Lord Jim* utters the motto *usque ad finem* ('Persevere to the very end'),[1] he is echoing a poignantly patriotic confession in one of Bobrowski's letters to his young nephew:

> I have gone through a lot, I have suffered over my own fate and the fate of my family and my Nation, and perhaps just because of these sufferings and disappointments I have developed in myself this calm outlook on the problem of life, whose motto, I venture to say, was, is, and will be 'usque ad finem'. The devotion to duty interpreted more widely or narrowly, according to circumstances and time – this constitutes my practical creed which – supported as it is by the experience of my sixty years – may be of some use to you?[2]

The economic basis of Conrad's early career is very clearly indicated in another letter that Bobrowski sent him: this letter was written in September of 1886, the year in which the errant nephew, after many years at sea, had qualified as a master in the merchant navy. I quote it at some length, for it well displays the intermingling of the economic and the literary in Conrad's background.

> The money [on this occasion £30 requested by Conrad] will probably arrive about a week late for it will take at least that time for it to reach Odessa and then be posted on to London. I am now just telling you that it will arrive, proving my constant solicitude for you. I do not know how much longer I shall be able to manifest my remembrance in such a tangible form. For if Hamlet said 'Something is rotten in the State of Denmark', so it has been the case for some time in our agricultural affairs. The fall in the prices of grain (in spite of the bad harvest this year our local needs can always be met) and sugar affects the rent one can get for one's land. The leaseholders are losing badly..... [W]hatever the price of land may be I am not going to farm it myself, so I shall let it for whatever it will fetch.....

The capital invested in the sugar refineries' shares brings me as little as 5% as compared with 30 and 35% in the past. A loss of capital may even follow. My source of income is thus threatened, and the remaining capital invested privately at 8%, however carefully invested, may be endangered as well as a result of the general poverty. As you see, the position is not to be envied and I can say with Hamlet 'something is rotten' while not, however, taking the matter as tragically as he did.[3]

Tadeusz Bobrowski's heavy emphasis on the bleakness of the economic climate is partly intended to chasten a sometimes feckless and extravagant nephew; and the concluding remark about not taking the matter as tragically as Hamlet tallies with Bobrowski's concern to control the melancholic and depressive side of Conrad's temperament. The ease with which the Shakespeare quotation came to the uncle's mind shows how culturally civilised was the milieu in which Conrad had grown up. The letter as a whole reminds us that the direct or indirect income from land was what enabled Bobrowski to sustain young Conrad's peripatetic and sometimes erratic progress through the world. The fields were let to tenant-farmers; from their profits on the sale of the wheat and sugar-beet, rent was paid to Bobrowski; and from that rent he was able to make investments in sugar-refineries and other commercial ventures. Bobrowski had also earmarked for Conrad half of his own inheritance from a relative, Mikołaj Bobrowski. In 1890, when Conrad visited him at Kazimierówka, Tadeusz presented his thirty-two-year-old nephew with the long and meticulous balance-sheet which is now known as 'The Bobrowski Document'. The entry for 1887 states:

In view of the fact that in November you will reach the age of thirty, by which time everyone ought to be self-supporting, and moreover because the education of the late Kazimierz's children is costing more, I told you that I must discontinue a regular allowance. This I intend to do and must do. *Thus the making of a man out of Mr. Konrad has cost* – apart from the 3,600 given you as capital ... 17,454 [roubles]. . . . .[4]

At that time, ten roubles were roughly equivalent to one English pound. So 'the making of a man out of Mr. Konrad' had cost, on Bobrowski's scrupulous reckoning, £1745, during a period in

which an English working man with a family would be fortunate
to earn £50 per year.

This was, of course, in addition to all the wages that Conrad
had earned (often at appreciable risk to his life) during his
arduous years at sea. Conrad had left Poland in 1874 at the age of
sixteen: he stayed first in Marseille, working intermittently as a
pilot and undertaking voyages to the West Indies. Subsequently
he travelled to England and served on a wide variety of ships,
from humble coasters to four-masted clippers, gaining experience,
passing examinations and accumulating qualifications. His wages
at sea were variable and often uncertain: they could be as low as
one shilling per month (on the *Skimmer of the Sea*) or as high as
£14 per month (on the *Otago*). Yet throughout that time his
financial security was guaranteed by the remittances from his
uncle. That Conrad had this form of economic insurance partly
accounts for his mobility in those years: he served for no longer
than two years on any one ship. It also accounts, in part, for his
distinctive manner and bearing: other seafarers referred to him as
'The Russian Count',[5] for, when going ashore, he stood out from
other captains by his aristocratic manner and dandified mode of
dress – dark jacket, light-coloured waistcoat, spruce trousers ('all
of these well made and of great elegance'), black or grey bowler
hat tilted to one side, gloves and a gold-topped Malacca cane.
When he eventually abandoned his maritime career for that of a
professional writer, the risks were somewhat reduced – indeed,
he was encouraged to take this step – by the knowledge that
when his old and ailing uncle died, Conrad would inherit a
substantial sum: in the event, £1600, which he received in the
year of publication of his first novel, *Almayer's Folly*. Subsequently,
for many years, Conrad floundered in financial difficulties, struggling to meet deadlines and to redeem debts, until the commercial
success of *Chance* in 1914 at last guaranteed his prosperity. There
are many reasons why Conrad turned to a novelist's career: the
need to resolve inner tensions and contradictions; the desire to
memorialise the beauty and strangeness of the world through
which he had voyaged; and the sense of solidarity with his
family's cultural milieu and with the time-defying community of
creative writers. In his lonely struggles as a writer, he sometimes
compared himself with a tightrope performer.[6] But during his
maritime years, and in the earliest phase of his literary career, he
was a tightrope performer aided by a financial safety-net which

had been extended by Uncle Tadeusz and which had been woven by tenant-farmers of the Polish soil and by workers in the sugar-beet mills. It is appropriate that in *Nostromo* Conrad would offer a masterly analysis of the relationship between idealistic aspirations and material interests, and would elaborate the irony that the complex apparatus of a modern state is sustained by the labours of illiterate peasants and sweaty mine-workers.

2.2.2 Polish Years

When Conrad's father, Apollo, married Ewa Bobrowska in 1856, Ewa brought with her a substantial dowry: 12 000 roubles (approximately £1200) and more than five kilogrammes of silver.[7] Apollo worked for some years, unsuccessfully, as an estate manager: his real enthusiasm was for creative writing and patriotic politics. Soon much of Ewa's dowry had been spent, and Apollo was helped by 2000 roubles (part of a bequest) supplied by Kazimierz Bobrowski, and subsequently by a further sum of 954 roubles (from another bequest) transmitted by Tadeusz Bobrowski, who also cleared some of Apollo's debts. When Conrad was a child, Tadeusz supplied 400 roubles per year (later increased to 500 and then 600) towards his upkeep, and his maternal grandmother provided additional funds. After Ewa's death, Tadeusz invested as capital for Conrad 250 roubles, the residue of her estate, together with 3750 roubles resulting from further legacies. The financial balance-sheet compiled by Tadeusz Bobrowski is lengthy and intricate, but what it makes clear is that whenever an emergency arose, Uncle Tadeusz was there to meet the emergency with money either from Conrad's inheritance or from his own income. This pattern continued throughout the uncle's lifetime. Another feature stressed by Bobrowski is that whereas the Korzeniowski side of Conrad's ancestry was characterised by romantic patriotism, a readiness to make sacrifices even in blood for the cause of Polish nationhood, the Bobrowski side, though patriotic, was determined to give prior claim to the nurturing of the family by careful curatorship of the lands and their incomes. Typically, it was Tadeusz Bobrowski who met Apollo Korzeniowski's funeral expenses.

From his father, Conrad imbibed romantic nationalism, the melancholy of defeated aspirations, and the example of intense dedication to literary work. From his uncle, who, after Apollo's death, was so dominant an influence, Conrad imbibed a spirit of sceptical rationalism and severe realism. Zdzisław Najder comments:

> To sympathize with Apollo's desperate determination to subordinate his whole life to a common cause one had to understand his reasons and to share, at least partly, his beliefs. Bobrowski did not share them and hardly ever tried to discover what had led Apollo to his extreme political views. . . . . But if Apollo's beliefs were seen as nonsensical or capricious, then his whole life, into which he had drawn his wife, must have appeared one of cruel folly.
>
> Thus his father's heritage was for Conrad a cause of strong internal conflict. . . . . Conrad's father must have seemed to him at once awe-inspiring and absurd; his attitude towards him was a mixture of admiration and contemptuous pity. And he could never forgive his father the death of his mother.[8]

The consequent ambivalence was to express itself in numerous ways in Conrad's fiction: repeatedly a wife or dependant suffers because of the exalted aspirations, dreams or visions of the husband. In *Nostromo*, for example, the theme is doubly emphasised: Gould's wife suffers for her husband's preoccupation with the silver which he believes will establish a civilised nation, while Viola's wife is embittered by Giorgio's unrewarded obsession with the dream of an independent republican Italy.

After his father's death, Conrad was cared for by a succession of family guardians. Any schooling that he received was intermittent and irregular; predominantly he was privately educated by a young tutor, Adam Marek Pulman. Conrad was a studious boy, reading widely and intensely, but also capricious, sensitive and egocentric, and delicate in health: he suffered migraines, stones in the bladder and possibly epilepsy. Indeed, when Uncle Tadeusz eventually acceded to his wish to go to sea, one of the main considerations was that sea air might be beneficial to his health. Another reason for Conrad's desire to travel abroad was practical and obliquely patriotic: as a Russian citizen by law, and as the son of a convict, Conrad would have been obliged to serve for possibly twenty-five years in the Russian Army had he remained at home.[9] Thirdly, there was the romantic appeal of seafaring (so strongly impressed on Conrad by his childhood reading of novels of adventure and travellers' memoirs) and the prospect of roaming far from a Poland synonymous with defeat and tragedy.

2.2.3 Maritime Career

After the sombre years in Poland came the contrast of southern
France, long hot summers and crowded colourful streets; Conrad's
four years in Marseille were among the most varied and adventurous of his whole career. Marseille in the 1870s was both a
bustling, thriving port and a cosmopolitan city, with its theatres,
operas and salons, its fashionable or bohemian restaurants, its
waterfront taverns. It was here, almost certainly, that Conrad
came to know the plays of Scribe and Sardou and the operas of
Meyerbeer, Offenbach and Bizet – *Carmen* was his favourite. His
later writings indicated that he entered an intense love-affair, and
at his age it would be surprising if he had not; and he made
friends easily, being popular with aristocrats and artists, sea-
captains and pilots.

In course of time he became an experienced pilot himself, being
paid a hundred francs each time he guided a ship into port. He
also made his first oceanic voyages. In 1874 he sailed for
Martinique as a passenger on the *Mont-Blanc*, a three-masted
barque of 394 tons; she returned to Marseille in May 1875, and
within a month Conrad re-embarked on her – this time as an
apprentice – for Saint-Pierre, again in the West Indies. From the
point of view of his subsequent fiction, the most important
voyage in this period was probably that made in 1876 on another
sailing-ship, the *Saint-Antoine*, for which he was paid 35 francs per
month as a steward. The first mate was a forty-two-year-old
Corsican, Dominic Cervoni, resourceful, bold and taciturn, who
became a prototype of Nostromo; the vessel called at Cartagena in
Colombia and Puerto Cabello and La Guaira in Venezuela, providing some scenic glimpses to be used in *Nostromo*; and a further
link with that novel is that the ship may have been smuggling
guns to the conservative rebels in Colombia.[10] In the autobiographical volume, *The Mirror of the Sea*, Conrad claimed that he
had also joined Dominic Cervoni in a syndicate which smuggled
arms from Marseille to Spain, using a small vessel called *Tremolino*
which was eventually wrecked after a pursuit by coastguards. In
both *The Mirror* and *The Arrow of Gold*, Conrad embellished and
glamorised this venture, but the probability remains that while
based in Marseille the young Conrad was indeed a runner of
contraband in the Mediterranean.[11]

Whatever his earnings from lawful and unlawful ventures,
Conrad spent prodigally. Tadeusz Bobrowski provided his

nephew with a generous allowance of 2000 francs per year; but, in the first half of 1876 alone, Conrad sought and obtained from the long-suffering uncle more than twice as much as his six-monthly allowance: 2465 francs. At this time a lieutenant in the French Navy would have been paid about 2000 francs per year, an industrial worker 800 to 900 francs, and a craftsman 1800 francs on average.[12] Tadeusz complained bitterly that Conrad was recklessly spending a substantial proportion of his uncle's total income.

> My income is around 5,000 roubles – I pay 500 roubles in taxes – by giving you 2,000 francs I am giving you approximately 700 roubles and to your Uncle [Kazimierz] 1,000 roubles yearly; so I give the two of you about one-third of my income.[13]

In addition to worries caused by his financial entanglements, Conrad learned to his dismay, in December 1877, that as a Russian subject he had no right to serve on French vessels without permission from the Russian Consul; and, since he was liable for military service in Russia, no consent would be forthcoming. (If Conrad sought to become naturalised as a *French* citizen, he would be liable for French military service.) Heavily in debt, Conrad borrowed 800 francs from a friend, went to Villefranche to try to join an American squadron, but failed, and in desperation gambled away the borrowed money at Monte Carlo. He returned to Marseille, put a pistol to his chest and pulled the trigger; the bullet went through his chest but missed the heart.[14] While he recovered, the long-suffering Tadeusz, summoned by telegram, arrived to tend his ward and to clear numerous debts totalling over 3000 francs. To a relative, Bobrowski reported of Conrad:

> My study of the Individual has convinced me that he is not a bad boy, only one who is extremely sensitive, conceited, reserved, and in addition excitable. In short I found in him all the defects of the Nałęcz family. He is able and eloquent . . . . . very popular with his captains and also with the sailors. . . . . In his ideas and discussions he is ardent and original . . . . . and is an imperialist. De gustibus non est disputandum [it is pointless to dispute about tastes].[15]

Finally, it was agreed that Conrad should join the British Merchant Navy, 'where there are no such formalities as in France';

so, on 10 June 1878, the apprentice seaman arrived at Lowestoft on the coal freighter *Mavis*.

In his letters to Conrad, Uncle Tadeusz repeatedly offered warnings that his nephew was a double man, an inheritor of a janiform personality. On his father's side, he had inherited an unstable temperament: changeable, imaginative, impatient, brooding, impractical; while, on his mother's side, he had inherited powers of patient diligence and steady application. Though Tadeusz exaggerated the contrast, Conrad's long phase as a seaman in the British Mercantile Marine was to illustrate this duplicity. He never stayed on any vessel for long, sometimes because of quarrels with his captains, sometimes for no evident reason (and to the disappointment of the owners); yet, on the other hand, his zeal and perseverence took him, by the age of thirty, to the pinnacle of a naval career.

His beginnings in England could not have been more humble. He obtained a berth on a small coaster, the barquentine *Skimmer of the Sea* which carried coal from Newcastle to Lowestoft; and the vessel's documents record Conrad's wage as one shilling per month, when even the ship's boy received twenty-five shillings. But here, he recalled, 'I began to learn English from East Coast chaps each built as though to last for ever, and coloured like a Christmas card.'[16] After *Skimmer*, he soon found a berth as an ordinary seaman on the wool clipper *Duke of Sutherland*, which plied between London and Sydney; and gradually, over the subsequent sixteen years, with numerous voyages on ships ranging from elegant three-masters to rusty tramp-steamers, he rose in rank: third mate, second mate, skipper. Repeatedly on the great ocean-going sailing ships he made the run between England, Bombay and Australia; steadily, struggling with the wayward English language, he learned the rules of seamanship and passed the successive inquisitorial examinations; and in 1886, he not only gained his master's certificate but also took British nationality. Bobrowski was delighted by the double achievement: he had long urged his nephew to relinquish Russian citizenship and become 'a free citizen of a free country'.[17] Conrad was now exempt from the obligation of Russian military service and had become a denizen of a nation approaching the zenith of imperial power – a nation which, as recently as the 1850s, had fought in the Crimea the Poles' most hated oppressors, the Russians. In the service of the British Empire, Conrad repeatedly voyaged across the globe: to Bombay, Singapore or Melbourne. This was the last great era of sail, of the full-rigged iron sailing ships like the *Tilkhurst* that carried jute from Calcutta to Dundee (Conrad was her second mate in 1886) or of majestic clippers like the *Torrens* that carried wool from Adelaide to London. On the *Torrens* Conrad, the first mate, met John Galsworthy, who was voyaging as a passenger, and thus began the long friendship between the two future novelists. On these journeys Conrad came to know the foaming seas and hot sunsets, the storms and calms which later he was to celebrate in his books; he came to know Singapore and Java, Sumatra and Borneo, regions which provided settings for *Lord Jim* and the early novels; he encountered those borderline areas of human experience where the civilised meets the primitive and the familiar confronts the alien. He also gained an intimate knowledge of work – monotonous, backbreaking, unremitting work as a crewman; the worries of responsibility as mate or captain; the fears of storm and fog at sea, or even the fear of fear.

On the *Palestine*, an old and decrepit barque on which he served as second mate, Conrad faced the risk of death by water and by fire. Having left Newcastle for Bangkok in 1882, carrying coals, she lost her sails in a gale, sprang a leak, and returned to England for repairs. At the second attempt she reached the Bangka Strait off Sumatra, but the coals smouldered, the coal-gas exploded, and the ship was then consumed by a mass of fire; Conrad and the crew reached the shore in open boats. Many years later, the *Palestine* was re-launched in the pages of 'Youth' as the *Judea*. Indeed, hindsight readily gives the impression that one of Conrad's motives during his maritime career was to glean experiences to sustain his subsequent career as a writer. In Singapore he heard about A. P. Williams, the seaman involved in scandal who tried to make good, and who became one of the models for Lord Jim. On a voyage to the Berau River in Borneo, Conrad met Charles Olmeijer, the trader whose fictional counterpart was the Almayer of *Almayer's Folly*. Then there was William Lingard, a formidable sea-rover who had fought pirates and knew the coastal waters better than any other European – the genitor of the Tom Lingard of *Almayer's Folly*, *An Outcast of the Islands* and *The Rescue*. At Singapore, Conrad met Captain Ellis, the laconic Master-Attendant of the harbour, who was to make brief appearances in *Lord Jim*, 'The End of the Tether' and *The Shadow-Line*. And it was at Bangkok in 1888 that Conrad took charge of his first command – the *Otago*, a 346-ton three-masted barque of elegantly beautiful proportions. There was disease (dysentery and cholera) among the crew, and his first voyage, from Bangkok to Singapore, took three weeks instead of the usual three days, for she was often becalmed; but out of Conrad's frustrations and anxieties would eventually be born one of his finest novels, *The Shadow-Line*.

Meanwhile, Conrad's progress in the merchant marine entailed a welcome reduction in worry for the long-suffering Uncle Tadeusz. In emergencies, or for special purposes like the cost of Conrad's naturalisation as a British citizen (£25), he was still ready to furnish funds; but in 1881 he felt able to halve Conrad's regular allowance to £50 per year, and in 1884 it was further reduced to £30. Conrad's wages as a seaman varied considerably from ship to ship, and there were periods between voyages when he was earning nothing. Nevertheless, as first mate on the *Highland Forest* at £7 per month, or on the *Torrens* at £8, or as master of the *Otago* at £14 per month, Conrad was enjoying a substantial income. At this time, an English bricklayer could expect to earn £6 per month,[18] but out of that sum the bricklayer would have to pay for his food and accommodation, whereas at sea, Conrad's food and accommodation would be available without charge; and, further-more, a voyage would provide the sometimes-prodigal seaman with few opportunities for expenditure. (From 1884 onwards an additional source of income was the trickle of dividends from the London-based shipping firm, Barr, Moering and Co. Bobrowski supplied approximately £350 – increased in 1889 to £750 – as Conrad's investment in this company, which also provided occa-sional employment as warehouse-manager for Conrad.) The com-bination of the private income from Poland and the wages from seamanship would enable Conrad to maintain a gentlemanly life-style when ashore: not affluent, but with a certain freedom for excursions and for meetings with well-to-do families; and, when based in England, he could sample the theatres and music-halls of London and make continental visits. The double income also entailed a double perspective: an intermittent sense of critical detachment from the demanding, strenuous and often perilous life at sea. Conrad also knew that when Uncle Tadeusz died, he stood to inherit the large sum of £1600; and it is not entirely coincidental that he received that inheritance in the year in which his first novel was accepted for publication. As Bobrowski ceased to be the regular provider of money, so, in 1894, Conrad accepted his first literary payment: £20 outright (no royalties) for *Almayer's Folly*. The book was dedicated 'To the Memory of T.B.'.

2.2.4 Basis of the Literary Career

In Australia in March 1889, after a one-sided love-affair in Mauritius, Conrad resigned his command of the *Otago* and return- ed as a steamship-passenger to England – to furnished rooms at Bessborough Gardens, near Vauxhall Bridge in central London; and it was in that riverside setting that at the age of thirty-one, with time on his hands while looking for another command, he began his first novel. The manuscript of *Almayer's Folly* was to accompany him on his travels for the next five years – a wad to be brooded over, to be forgotten for a while, then to be pulled out for additions and revisions. It accompanied him into the Congo in 1890, during the depressing venture from which Conrad returned to recuperate from dysentery and malaria; and on the *Torrens* in 1891 he read part of it to a dying passenger, E. H. Jacques, who assured him that the novel was worth finishing. Then in 1894, when Conrad joined the *Adowa* as second mate, the ship's voyage was cancelled, and he learned of Bobrowski's death. In that lull, *Almayer's Folly* was completed and was despatched to the publish- ing house of T. Fisher Unwin, where W. H. Chesson recommended its acceptance for publication. When the book appeared in 1895, Conrad immediately became a widely-reviewed author. The re- views were mixed: some were scathing, some enthusiastic; but they were numerous, and clearly indicated that a strangely distinc- tive writer had emerged.

Conrad's transition from the capstan to the writing-desk was to be gradual and wavering: as late as 1898, with several novels and tales in print, he visited ship-owners in Glasgow in the hope of securing a command. It is clear, however, that numerous factors in this period were pushing him away from the sea and towards the literary life. To begin with, though Conrad was well qualified and adequately experienced as a master, it was increasingly difficult for him to gain posts commensurate with his qualifications. Long-distance sailing ships were becoming larger and more efficient, so fewer masters were needed; and steamships were steadily superseding sailing vessels (by 1894, two-thirds of the total tonnage of the British merchant fleet were transported by steam), so that Conrad, whose experience was predominantly with vessels under sail, was at a disadvantage. Between 1875 and 1894 the total tonnage of British shipping had risen from 6 153 000 to 8 956 000; but in the same period the number of vessels registered with the British Merchant Navy had diminished from 25 461 to 21 206; and of the sailing ships in this number, there had been a steep decline from 21 291 to 12 943.[19] Not only was it the case that on average 260 masters were becoming unemployed each year,[20] but also conditions at sea were deteriorating: ships were under-manned, while crews were often ill-trained and under-paid. Loss of life in shipwreck was a common daily occurrence: of the first seven British vessels on which Conrad sailed, no fewer than five were lost during a four-year period. Conrad's prospects in the merchant marine became gradually more daunting; and by late 1890 he was physically and mentally debilitated by the dispiriting ordeal of the Congo, and bruised by years of danger and discomfort. Furthermore, as Ian Watt suggests, 'the social and intellectual disparities between himself and the average ship's officer must also have become increasingly evident'.[21]

In turn, the pressures towards a literary career were both personal and circumstantial. First, there was the love of literature instilled in Conrad from childhood, particularly from those days when the world of fiction offered a consoling refuge from domestic gloom and grief. Secondly, there was familial example, which was multiple. Apollo Korzeniowski had gained fame as a poet, playwright and translator, and Uncle Tadeusz had subsequently urged Conrad to use his travels as material for descriptive articles which might be published in Poland (while Tadeusz himself had steadily been compiling the acerbic memoirs which were to be published posthumously). Then there was the example and encouragement of Conrad's 'aunt', Marguerite Poradowska. She lived in Brussels and was the widow of Aleksander Poradowski, the first cousin of Conrad's maternal grandmother. Conrad's correspondence with her began in 1890 and continued for many years; sometimes the tone was amatory, and Bobrowski warned his nephew against an intimate involvement with the widow:

[A]s an old sparrow friendly to you both I advise you to give up this game, which will end in nothing sensible. A worn-out female, and if she is to join up with somebody, it will be with Buls [Charles Buls, burgomaster of Brussels] who would give her a position and love. . . . .[22]

In the early 1890s she was pursuing a literary career with some success: Conrad read and praised her tales and novels, and enthusiastically discussed her evolving literary projects. Undoubtedly her example encouraged him to persevere with *Almayer's Folly*, and he was prompt to tell her of its completion:

> J'ai la douleur de Vous faire part de la mort de M. Kaspar Almayer qui a eu lieu ce matin a 3^h [I regret to inform you of the death of Mr Kaspar Almayer, which took place at 3 o'clock this morning].[23]

In addition, the early years of their correspondence had provided a testing-ground for Conrad's ideas and style: to Poradowska he offered paragraphs of sceptical, pessimistic, sometimes self-pitying analysis in which already some of the characteristic rhythms of Conradian rhetoric can be heard. The correspondence is in French, but when Conrad inveighs against 'the doctrine (or theory) of atonement through suffering' ('tout simplement une infâme abomination quand des gens civilisés la prêchent')[24] the sardonic tones of *Nostromo*'s Decoud are anticipated; and we hear already the urbanely bleak scepticism of the Marlow of 'Heart of Darkness' in the passage which declares 'que l'on ne devient utile que quand on [a] realisé toute l'etendue de l'insignificance de l'individu dans l'arrangement de l'univers' ['One becomes useful only after recognising the full extent of the individual's insignificance in the arrangement of the universe'].[25] Raymond Williams has coined the term 'negative identification' for that process of vicarious self-pity whereby an author sees in some disadvantaged social group (the rural poor or the suffering proletariat) a mirror of the author's own apparently unfortunate plight;[26] the letters to Marguerite Poradowska show Conrad's plangent self-pity modulating into a philosophical form of that negative identification – a keen sense of the woes of sensitive individuals in a largely hostile social world and within a bleakly inhuman immensity of the cosmos.

British imperial expansion in the nineteenth century had created the conditions in which Conrad could gain employment on ocean-going vessels; it also helped to create the potential readership for his novels and tales. Publishers knew that there was a vast market at home for factual and fictional accounts of exotic regions, of daring exploration, of 'outposts of progress'. Rider Haggard was gaining wealth from his novels of Africa, Kipling from his novels and tales of India; and Conrad saw that the Malay Archipelago might become his own distinctive territory for fictional exploration. Maritime writing, too, whether by Melville, R. H. Dana or Clark Russell, was of proven appeal. And a novelist in England in the 1890s could enjoy a peculiarly fortunate combination of circumstances.

In the first place there was the enormous expansion of education in Victorian England. As the electorate of a soaring population was increased by the 1832 and particularly the 1867 Reform Bills, so governments saw the merits of 'civilising' the electorate by educational reform; the Education Act of 1870, for example, established locally-elected school boards which could compel attendance to the age of thirteen (fees being waived for poor parents) and which were empowered to build new schools maintained in part by local rates, while existing Church schools received increased grants. During the subsequent twenty years a huge school-building programme proceeded. Publishing houses multiplied to supply the needs of an increasing readership; a diversity of magazines flourished. At the census of 1881, 3400 respondents identified themselves as authors, editors or journalists; by 1891, the figure was 6000; by 1901, 11000.[27] Publishers could exploit quite systematically the class strata. A first edition of a novel (perhaps a handsomely-bound six-shilling volume) would be aimed mainly at middle- and upper-middle-class readers, either by direct sale or via the libraries. If it sold reasonably well, a cheap reprint might subsequently cater for a humbler readership; and eventually, when that market was exhausted, there might appear an even cheaper reprint for the railway bookstalls. Victorian readers were remarkably well served by libraries. Legislation passed in 1850 had given local authorities the power to establish free public libraries funded by rate-payers; commercial circulating libraries like Mudie's could distribute books by post even to those subscribers who lived in remote parts of Britain; semi-private subscription-libraries like the London Library (which Conrad joined in 1897) could provide good research-facilities and the atmosphere of a scholarly club-room; and the clubs themselves (like the Junior Carlton, where Galsworthy would see fellow members requesting *The Nigger of the 'Narcissus'*) stocked current novels.[28]

Another development which proved to be of vast importance for Conrad was the movement for international regulation of copyright, and, in particular, the signing in 1891 of the first copyright agreement between Britain and the United States: the Chace Act. Before that time, British authors were regularly pirated in the USA; at best, they could expect only occasional 'courtesy payments' from the American publishers. But, after 1891, an author could be paid twice over for the same novel: first by its British publisher and secondly by its American publisher. Indeed, it was quite possible for a novel to earn four or more payments, in the following way. A publisher who owned a magazine (Blackwood, for example, or Heinemann), would pay the author for the serialisation of the work; an American magazine in contact with the British publishing house would also serialise it, again paying the author; then the first book edition would appear in Britain, while nearly-simultaneous publication of the book would take place in the USA; and, in course of time, there might be cheaper reprints on both sides of the Atlantic. All this would be in addition to 'Imperial' publication and to continental editions in translation or (as in the case of Tauchnitz texts) in English. When one looks back over the years, the 1890s resemble a golden age for aspiring writers, given the enormous number of magazines (some venerable and distinguished, others new and popular, others radical and avant-garde) which readily published novels, tales and literary essays. Furthermore, a novelist could gain unprecedented attention from reviewers: not only were there so many periodicals reviewing new literary work, but also those reviews were often far more lengthy and detailed than would be possible fifty or more years later. If we consult *Conrad: The Critical Heritage*, which reprints reviews of Conrad's books, a striking feature is the abundance of attention that he received at the start of his career; furthermore that volume reprints only a small selection, and by no means the totality; and even then, its editor is often obliged to curtail or condense the reviews by omitting their detailed citations of the text and summaries of the plot. Another factor was that magazine payments were often handsome: for instance, in November 1897 *Blackwood's* sent Conrad £40 for the short tale, 'Karain': twice the amount initially earned by Conrad's first novel – and twice the sum that Conrad's maid was to earn by a year's work in 1900.[29] It is salutary to recall that between 1865 and 1905, Henry James's earnings from serialisation of his works greatly exceeded the income from their book versions.[30] Publishers believed that prior publication in magazines could improve the prospects of a forthcoming book by serving as an elaborate form of publicity which would keep an author's name in the public eye over an extended period, and which would also generate publicity in journals prepared to review periodical fiction alongside books.[31]

Conrad's career would often give instances of ways in which it would be possible for a writer, when reasonably well established in reputation, to be paid numerous times for the same manuscript of a work of fiction. In addition to the fees for serialisation in Great Britain and the United States, there could be advance payments and royalties for the initial book publications, royalties on cheaper reprints, fees for foreign English-language editions and translations, a further sum for the incorporation of the work in a 'Collected Edition', and eventually payment for film rights and the purchase of the manuscript by an astute collector. Of course, in his early years as a novelist Conrad underwent anguished struggles and was repeatedly in debt; of course, his letters give memorable and moving expression to his sense of conflict between what he wants to create and what the public will buy; but still he survived as an artist, and eventually he was to prosper enormously. And an aspiring novelist who could compare notes and exchange complaints with Henry James, H. G. Wells, Stephen Crane, John Galsworthy and R. B. Cunninghame Graham could hardly complain of neglect by his professional fraternity.

The list of Conradian publications given in the 'Chronological Table' of this book is designed to emphasise several points. The first is that when, today, we look at a collected edition of Conrad's works, we see only a part of his total output. The collected edition does not display all the variant forms in which his work appeared. It does not display, for example, the serial version of *The Secret Agent*, or the dramatisation, or the many significant differences between the various editions and impressions. The serialisations of *Under Western Eyes* and *Chance* are much *longer* than the familiar book-texts; and the *Forum* magazine text of 'The Duel' (there entitled 'The Point of Honor') is intermittently superior to the now-familiar version in *A Set of Six*.[32] The 'Chronological Table' also seeks to show that, in his lifetime, one of Conrad's rôles was that of literary journalist: a contributor of serials, tales, essays, polemics and topical articles to magazines and newspapers. He may then be seen by us less as a member of an élite (the authors of profound texts for academic exegesis) and more as an entertainer and communicator, a man prepared to speak through popular newspapers and magazines like the *Daily Mail* and *Réveille* as well as through *Cosmopolis* and the *English Review*. One section of *The Mirror of the Sea* first appeared in *Blackwood's*, others in the *Daily Mail*, the *Standard*, *Harper's Weekly*, *Pall Mall* and *World Today*. Not only did such widespread publication enhance Conrad's income; it also acted as a permeating publicity, making his name known to typists reading penny newspapers as well as businessmen scanning illustrated weeklies, and thus prepared the way for his eventual emergence as an author who was both prestigious and popular, a sage who was an inspiring celebrity

3

Cultural

From 1895 onwards, Conrad rapidly made his mark in England as a powerfully original writer. One reason for that originality was the exceptional breadth of his cultural heritage. The ensuing sections give samples – samples only – of that heritage.

3.1 POLISH INFLUENCES

To the end of his life, notwithstanding the long domicile in England, Conrad spoke English with a marked Polish accent; and though he soon achieved an astonishing linguistic eloquence in his writings, they still bore occasional signs (a lapse into a Polish idiom here or a French construction there) that English was not his native language. He told Garnett in 1908: 'I had to work like a coal-miner in his pit quarrying all my English sentences out of a black night.'[1] Artists are skilled at converting apparent liabilities into assets. In Conrad's case, the fact that he was writing in a foreign language can clearly be related to one of the most striking features of his supreme works, 'Heart of Darkness' and *Nostromo*. Repeatedly these texts manifest a linguistic scepticism which anticipates the subsequent concerns of philosophers like Wittgenstein, Sartre and Derrida. Conrad sardonically depicts the contrasts between word and fact, notion and nature, creed and deed, preaching and practice. And since Conrad's art, at best, constantly aspires to the condition of paradox, what he offers is a critical anticipation of that later scepticism. Typically, Marlow in 'Heart of Darkness' sounds eloquent warnings against eloquence, vividly describes intense experiences while asserting that words are inadequate vehicles of intense experience, and explains in persuasive language that language generates illusions which bring sustenance or servitude.

Similarly, to Conrad's upbringing in a beleaguered Poland can be related the fact that in his day he was the most acutely perceptive of political novelists. He understood both the glamour of imperialism and its hypocrisy; both the Titanism of economic expansion and the sordid realities of 'material interests'. And his Polish years had taught him that artistic creation can, simultaneously, be political action.

These claims are illustrated in the following survey of some of the Poles who contributed to Conrad's literary career.

Apollo Korzeniowski

In *A Personal Record*, Conrad claimed that his first acquaintance with English literature came when, as a child sharing his parents' exile in Siberia, he read some pages of Shakespeare's *Two Gentlemen of Verona* in his father's translation. Apollo Korzeniowski was fluent in English and French, translating not only several plays by Shakespeare but also Dickens' *Hard Times*, Alfred de Vigny's *Chatterton*, and various plays and novels of Victor Hugo. (Conrad said that his introduction to sea-literature was provided by his father's version of Hugo's *Les Travailleurs de la mer*.) Apollo's version of *Chatterton* was long regarded as the best Polish rendering of de Vigny's tragedy.[2]

There were various Polish political factions: the 'appeasers', who were willing to cooperate with the partitioning authorities; the Whites, who believed in national independence but advocated gradual and peaceful progress towards that goal; and the Reds, who advocated insurrectionary activity. Apollo actively supported the Reds and was also a disciple of the Polish Messianic movement, which claimed that Poland had a divinely-ordained historic mission: as Christ had suffered and died for humanity before being resurrected, so the Polish state had been destined to suffer in the cause of liberty but would eventually rise again to free nationhood. Although Apollo's patriotism left an enduring imprint on his son's imagination, Conrad seems, on the whole, to have reacted against his father's devoutly religious spirit. At Christmas 1920 he wrote to Edward Garnett:

> It's strange how I always, from the age of fourteen, disliked the Christian religion, its doctrines, ceremonies and festivals. . . . . [N]obody – not a single Bishop of them – believes in it. The business in the stable isn't convincing. . . . .[3]

Nevertheless Conrad's views, in his letters, were often inflected towards those of the addressee: if he was toughly sceptical in letters to sceptics like Garnett and Cunninghame Graham, he was also capable of offering pious exhortations to Ted and Helen Sanderson. Conrad's wife was a Catholic, and both his sons were brought up in that faith; and when he was invited to join a club for Anglicans, he replied: 'I was born a R.C. and though dogma sits lightly on me I have never renounced that form of Christian religion.'[4] Conrad's collaborator, F. M. Hueffer, was another Roman Catholic.

Apollo Korzeniowski's own works include sequences of poems which lament the failure of the 1848 revolution and scornfully upbraid the Polish gentry and their materialism:

> Noblemen-pedlars, Noblemen-sugarmongers,
> sheep-farmers, chapmen, merchants, beermongers;
> friends of the Government which lets you
> drain the people's blood
> under the protection of the Russian whip;
> evil bodies – muddy spirits;
> in your health is the people's sickness!
>   Begone! for I prefer,
> O probity, your bread, though it be dry![5]

Although his poems circulated widely in manuscript, his best-known work was a sequence of plays: *Komedia* (*Comedy*) written in 1855; *Dla miłego grosza* (*For the Sake of Money*), 1857–8; and *Bez ratunku* (*Without Help*), first published in 1866. All three maintain the themes of patriotic idealism and of contempt for the Polish commercial classes. *Komedia* endured best: in the 1950s it was praised by Roman Taborski and Jan Kott for its realism and politically 'progressive' features.[6] In his political journalism, Apollo reiterated that 'manufacture, industry and commerce should not overwhelm our agriculture, but should be subordinated to it', and that Russia is synonymous with barbaric servitude:

> From the time of the Ruriks onwards, under the Tartar yoke, under the tyranny of the Ivanovs, under the knouts of Tzars and Tzaritas, etc., she was, is and always will be a prison, otherwise she would cease to be herself. – In this prison perpetrated crimes and flourishing falsehood copulate

whorishly. The law and the established religion bless this union. Its progeny: the prostitution of all religious, social, political, national and personal relationships.[7]

Forty-one years later, a similar invective was given new resonance in Joseph Conrad's 'Autocracy and War' (1905):

> The Government of Holy Russia, arrogating to itself the supreme power to torment and slaughter the bodies of its subjects like a God-sent scourge, has been most cruel to those whom it allowed to live under the shadow of its dispensation. The worst crime against humanity of that system we behold now crouching at bay behind vast heaps of mangled corpses is the ruthless destruction of innumerable minds. . . . . [F]rom the very inception of [Russia's] being the brutal destruction of dignity, of truth, of rectitude, of all that is fruitful in human nature has been made the imperative condition of her existence.[8]

Like father, like son: to both, Poland seemed an outpost of western Europe, defending democracy, justice and liberty, whereas Russia stood for Asiatic tyranny and barbarism. The association of Muscovy with servitude is centuries old, has ample historical warrant, and is no prerogative of Poles alone: to Elizabethans, 'slave-born' was a stock epithet for Muscovites; later, Defoe portrayed the paganism and savagery of the inhabitants; and Karl Marx declared that 'Muscovy was raised and educated in the vicious and miserable school of Mongolian slavery'. In a speech of 1867, Marx added:

> There is but one alternative for Europe. Either Asiatic barbarism, under Muscovite direction, will burst around its head like an avalanche, or else it must re-establish Poland, thus putting twenty million heroes between itself and Asia. . . . .[9]

Furthermore, as Andrzej Busza has pointed out, Joseph Conrad's *Under Western Eyes* might even be deemed the completion of a project meditated by Apollo Korzeniowski in 1868: the writing of a novel 'about the corruption that has fallen upon us from Muscovy, through its Asiatic pomp, through its bureaucratic honours, the unbelief disseminated by its public educational system; further, through the baubles of the civilised, Muscovite high society. . . . .'[10]

Of course, it can be argued that since Conrad was only eleven years old at the time of his father's death, estimations of Apollo's influence may be exaggerated. There is no doubt, however, that the young Conrad was keenly aware of, and interested in, his father's work as a writer; that Apollo exerted a strong formative influence, particularly as Conrad had little orthodox schooling and was educated largely at home; and that, after Apollo's death, Conrad still had opportunities to read his father's work. Apollo was not a major Polish writer, but a significant one, famed in his lifetime; and from him Conrad imbibed a keen sense of the harmony between creation and translation, of the interconnection of serious writing and politics, a pessimism about progress, a scepticism about commercialism, and an enduring hostility to Russia. Indeed, in the light of Conrad's early upbringing and the bitter experience of Siberian exile, it is the very scrupulousness of the treatment of Russian matters in *Under Western Eyes* and in 'The Warrior's Soul' which seems the remarkable achievement.

Tadeusz Bobrowski

While Apollo was romantic, brooding, impetuous and quixotic, Conrad's guardian-uncle Tadeusz was pragmatic, circumspect and sceptical. Busza records that Bobrowski 'alienated the reactionaries by his social views and the radicals by his political outlook':

A fervent admirer of the French Revolution, he was deeply contemptuous of the Polish aristocracy and the higher gentry, and constantly sneered at their stupidity, conceit and snobbishness. He devoted much of his life to the cause of the peasantry. Having freed the serfs on his own estates, as soon as he came into his father's inheritance, he became one of the leaders of the emancipation movement in the Polish Ukraine. But his radicalism was strictly limited. He eyed with suspicion all new social developments and detested 'professional revolutionaries'.[11]

Though deeply patriotic, he felt that the journey to national independence should be slow and careful; he shared with the Polish positivists the view that a prime aim should be to increase the material wealth of Poland in order to regenerate its social structure; armed conflict with Russia was futile. (One is reminded of Charles Gould's belief, in *Nostromo*: 'Only let the material interests once get a firm footing, and they are bound to impose the conditions on which alone they can continue to exist..... A better justice will come afterwards. That's your ray of hope.') Indeed, he belonged to the very class of 'noblemen-sugarmongers' repeatedly assailed by Apollo. Bobrowski's own literary ambitions were limited to the compilation of the *Memoirs* which appeared posthumously in 1900, but he was a prodigious reader; one contemporary describes him thus:

> He was a solitary man ..... who had lost not only all his brothers and sisters, but also his wife and daughter..... He did not personally occupy himself with farming, preferring to rent his farms instead..... Weeks on end, he would stay at home, with a long chibouk [Turkish pipe] in his hand, surrounded by books and periodicals, always busy.....[12]

We have seen that Bobrowski's financial aid facilitated both Conrad's maritime career and his transition to literary work. But there is no doubt that Bobrowski also contributed to the complexities of Conrad's thought (and thus to the need to resolve tensions through literary creation) by emphasising and even exaggerating the contrast between the prudently diligent character of the Bobrowskis and the imaginatively wayward character of the Korzeniowskis:

> From the blending of the blood of these two excellent races in your worthy person should spring a character whose endurance and wise enterprise will cause the whole world to be astonished![13]

Repeatedly, in his long letters of advice, Tadeusz sounded the themes that were to re-echo in his protégé's works; as when, rebuking Conrad for a predictable jeremiad, he wrote:

> My dear lad, whatever you were to say about a good or bad balance of the forces of nature, about good or bad social relationships, about right or wrong social systems, about the boundless stupidity of crowds fighting for a crust of bread – and ending up in nothingness – none of this will be new!! You will never control the forces of nature, for whether blind or governed by Providence, in each case they have their own pre-ordained paths..... Certainly humanity has a lesser need of

producing geniuses than of the already-existing modest and
conscientious workers who fulfil their duties; nobody has the
right to call himself the former until he has proved it by deeds,
just as nobody has the right to withdraw from the work of the
latter because of his conviction that he is not part of the
team. . . . . So that if both Individuals and Nations were to make
'duty' their aim, instead of the ideal of greatness, the world
would certainly be a better place than it is! And those crowds
'aiming instinctively at securing only bread', so detestable to all
visionaries, have their raison d'être: to fulfil the material needs
of life; and they no longer seem detestable when, as often
happens, a more thorough evaluation reveals that they embellish
their existence, their work, and often even their shortcomings,
by some higher moral ideal of a duty accomplished, of a love
for their family or country. . . . .[14]

In the light of such letters, one could argue that *The Nigger of the
'Narcissus'*, for example, is a thematic battleground in which the
pessimism of Apollo Korzeniowski does battle with the faith in
duty and work represented by Tadeusz Bobrowski. And there are
other themes sounded in the Bobrowski correspondence which
resonate later in Conrad's fiction. Scepticism about language, for
example:

If the Prince of Benevento of 'accursed memory' was right
when he said that: 'Speech (in this case the written word) was
given us to conceal our thoughts', then, Panie Bracie, you have
coped most efficiently with the task. . . . .[15]

Many years later, the narrator of *Under Western Eyes* would report
of Razumov: 'The epigrammatic saying that speech has been
given to us for the purpose of concealing our thoughts came into
his mind.'[16] Bobrowski also expounded at length what eventually
would become a major thesis of *Lord Jim* – that imagination is both
blessing and curse, the source of dreams and of nightmares:

In your projects you let your imagination run away with you –
you become an optimist; but when you encounter disappointments you fall easily into pessimism – and as you have a lot of
pride, you suffer more as the result of disappointments than
somebody would who had a more moderate imagination but

was endowed with greater endurance in activity and relationships. . . . .[17]

W. B. Yeats wrote in *Mythologies* that 'We make out of the quarrel with others, rhetoric, but out of the quarrel with ourselves, poetry'.[18] One of Conrad's great motives in his fiction was a resolution of the quarrel between the Korzeniowski and the Bobrowski temperaments; another was self-vindication before the shades of the idealistically patriotic father and the demandingly scrupulous uncle.

Apollo, by his labours as translator, poet and playwright, had manifested the fascination and importance of literary endeavour; but he had never been a travel-writer. The suggestion that Conrad's maritime travels might supply materials for publication was made by Tadeusz Bobrowski:

> As thank God you do not forget your Polish (may God bless you for it, as I bless you) and your writing is not bad, I repeat what I have already written and said before – you would do well to write contributions for the *Wędrowiec* [a weekly magazine] in Warsaw. We have few travellers, and even fewer genuine correspondents: the words of an eyewitness would be of great interest and in time would bring you in money. It would be an exercise in your native tongue . . . . . and finally a tribute to the memory of your father who always wanted to and did serve his country by his pen. Think about this, young man, collect some reminiscences. . . . .[19]

Appropriately, then, when Conrad eventually turned his travel experiences into the material of novels, Bobrowski in various guises seems to inhabit that fictional universe. In *Lord Jim*, it is not simply Bobrowski's motto, *usque ad finem*, that has been transferred to Stein; for Stein's affectionate but partly critical attitude to Jim (the stance of a benevolent uncle who from afar, by money and by introductions, hopes to stabilise the career of a sometimes dreamy, impractical and even suicidal protégé) has distinct analogies with Bobrowski's attitude to his nephew. Indeed, a theme of 'hopeful guardians and wayward protégés' is important and recurrent in Conrad's novels from the outset of his fictional career. Lingard and Almayer; Lingard and Willems; Belfast and James Wait; Stein, Marlow and Lord Jim; Giorgio Viola and Nostromo;

Prince K— and Razumov; Mrs Fyne and Flora de Barral: the pattern is insistent. Jocelyn Baines suggested in 1960 that we may detect a covert expression of Conrad's rebelliousness against his father in those novels and tales (*Almayer's Folly, An Outcast of the Islands, Chance* and others) in which a young woman rebels against a father or stepfather;[20] but the tension between the temperaments of Joseph Conrad and his anxious guardian may also have found expression in the depiction of the youthful protégé who rebels against the mentor–patron.

In Conrad's writing there are some local and specific debts to Bobrowski's *Memoirs*: the reported description of Conrad's mother in *A Personal Record* is an edited version of Bobrowski's pen-portrait of her, while the tale 'Prince Roman' utilises the account in *Memoirs* of Prince Roman Sanguszko's confrontation with the Russian authorities.[21] But when such local debts have been considered, one has only to turn back to the long and moving sequence of Bobrowski's letters in order to feel that the most extensive literary debt was to Bobrowski's personality: for Uncle Tadeusz consistently advocated – and manifested in his guardianship – those principles of duty, fidelity and conscientious application to the task which became salient points of moral reference in Conrad's literary works.

Adam Mickiewicz and Juliusz Słowacki

'My father read *Pan Tadeusz* aloud to me and made me read it out loud on many occasions', Conrad recalled.[22] The greatest Polish writer is undoubtedly Adam Mickiewicz (1798–1855), author of the poem of historic legend, *Konrad Wallenrod* (1828), the drama *Dziady* (*Forefather's Eve*, 1832), and the splendid national epic, *Pan Tadeusz* (1832–4). When Joseph Conrad was baptized Józef Teodor Konrad Korzeniowski, the name Konrad was chosen largely for its patriotic literary associations. In Mickiewicz's *Dziady* the hero changes his name, formerly Gustavus, when he awakens to a mystical sense of his power to free Poland from Muscovite tyranny: he declares, 'Gustavus obiit. . . . . Hic natus est Conradus' – 'Gustavus is dead. . . . . Here Conrad is born'.[23] In *Konrad Wallenrod*, the eponymous hero is the leader of the Teutonic Crusaders – but he proves to be a Lithuanian Pole who had cunningly gained that leadership in order to guide his German followers into a completely disastrous campaign against Lithuania. The poem thus expresses an idea which would later so frequently preoccupy the novelist Joseph Conrad: the seeming paradox that loyalty often entails betrayal. Here loyalty to one's native land is seen by Wallenrod as justifying treachery to one's trusting followers; the patriotic end justifies the ruthlessly duplicitous means. Mickiewicz's endorsement of 'treacherous patriotism' is, however, strongly qualified. The protagonist is seen as a brooding, bitter figure, rendered harsh and saturnine by his duplicitous ambition; he declares:

> Hundred times
> Be cursed that hour in which, constrained by foes,
> I seize these means[;][24]

and, as his treachery becomes evident to the Teutonic knights, he cries:

> Wearied of treasons, I am unfit for war.
> Enough of vengeance. Germans, too, are men!
> God has enlightened me.[25]

When the knights approach to kill him, Konrad commits suicide by poison. In this concern with the psychological burden of patriotic treachery, *Konrad Wallenrod* foreshadows Conrad's *Under Western Eyes*; and a feature of Mickiewicz's poem which anticipates a typical Conradian technique is that the narrative contains various 'tales within the tale', all of which sound in different keys the theme of betrayal and patriotism.

Pan Tadeusz, too, maintains this theme. The epic's protagonist, Jacek Soplica, had once loved the daughter of a wealthy and loyal Polish magnate; when the magnate rejected his suit, Soplica killed him, thus helping the Russian foe. Subsequently Soplica was tortured both by his own conscience and by the general suspicion that he was a traitor. To atone for his crime, he first joins the Polish legions fighting under Napoleon, and secondly becomes a monk known as Father Robak (*'robak'* being Polish for 'worm' – an appropriate name for an underground worker). At the end of the poem, it is revealed that Father Robak has been acting as a secret agent, helping the French and Polish armies in their advance against the Russians. Thus, some features of Robak's story anticipate features of Lord Jim's and Razumov's, and particularly of Dr Monygham's in *Nostromo*. There is also a tenuous connection with 'Prince Roman', in which a man's grief at the loss of a beloved woman is slowly converted into a determination to fight self-sacrificially for Polish independence. Though partly historical, 'Prince Roman' is certainly embellished with literary details, for Yankel, its patriotic Jewish innkeeper, is a close counterpart of Jankiel (pronounced 'Yankiel') in *Pan Tadeusz*: they are similar in rôle, abode and physical appearance.[26]

As a child, Conrad was able to recite from memory Mickiewicz's ballads; and one of those ballads, 'Czaty' ('The Ambush') has a distinct relationship to Conrad's early Malay tale, 'Karain' (1897).[27] In 'Czaty', a Polish governor finds that his wife has taken a lover; the governor and his henchman, a Cossack, prepare an ambush for the couple; but the Cossack, pitying the wife, then shoots his master. In 'Karain', two Malays, Pata Matara and his friend Karain, ambush Matara's sister and a Dutchman with whom she has eloped. Karain, who has become infatuated with the woman's beauty, then shoots his friend instead of the European. Thus both narratives feature a double betrayal; in both, the appeal of the woman subverts the bond of loyalty between two men, and a determined avenger perishes at the hand of his trusted companion. In this respect, 'Czaty' offers a pre-echo of the violent climax of Conrad's novel *Victory*.

'Later I preferred Słowacki [to Mickiewicz],' said Conrad. 'You know why Słowacki? Il est l'âme de toute la Pologne, lui. [That man is the soul of all Poland].'[28] The works of Juliusz Słowacki (1809–49) are extremely diverse, varying from lyrical descriptive poems to satirical dramas; he was celebrated for 'literary cocktails' which combined elements of Shakespeare, Calderón, Lope de Vega and old Polish ballads. For much of his career Słowacki wrote in conscious rivalry with Mickiewicz; and the Konrad of Mickiewicz's *Dziady* has his critical counterpart in the eponymous hero of Słowacki's *Kordian* – the name is a part-anagram of Konrad. Kordian is neurotic, introspective; and the play (in Czesław Miłosz's view)

> magnifies the emotional capacity for revolutionary *élan* displayed by the Warsaw crowds, but the mob's political immaturity and the general lack of wise leaders comes in for sharp satire.[29]

Conrad's admiration for Słowacki may therefore have provided a useful grounding in political scepticism for the eventual author of *Nostromo*.

Henryk Sienkiewicz

During the 1880s Henryk Sienkiewicz, the Polish novelist and story-writer, had begun to establish an international reputation: though he wrote in Polish, his works had been translated into French and German. Then, in English-speaking nations, what has been termed an 'unintentional conspiracy of silence'[30] was broken by Scotland: *Blackwood's Magazine* published in April 1889 an unsigned article entitled 'A Polish Novelist – Henryk Sienkiewicz'.[31] Its writer complained that Polish literature, although 'immeasurably superior to that of Russia', had been remarkably neglected in the West. Few people in Britain, he said, knew the names of Poles like Słowacki and Korzeniowski, even though they deserved to be as widely known as were Dumas and Turgenev. In particular, he eulogised Sienkiewicz for combining the merits of Dumas, Turgenev and Bret Harte.

The alleged neglect of Sienkiewicz soon ended: in 1890, 1892 and 1893 appeared the English translations of the three parts of his *Trilogy* (*With Fire and Sword, The Deluge, Pan Michael*), and these panoramic historical novels of Polish struggles received wide and generally laudatory attention from critics in the United States and (to a lesser extent) in Great Britain. A reviewer in the *Literary News*[32] claimed that Sienkiewicz had achieved for Poland what Dumas had for France and Wagner for Germany: he had won international recognition of his nation's history. Sienkiewicz's popularity reached its zenith when the translation of *Quo Vadis* was published in 1896: speedily this saga of the rise of Christianity in ancient Rome reached the best-seller lists in the USA; and in 1900 the stage version opened in both New York and London. By 1901, the President of Johns Hopkins University could declare in Kraków, 'America thanks Poland for three great names: Copernicus, ... Kościuszko, ... and Sienkiewicz, whose name is a household word'.[33] And in 1905 Sienkiewicz was awarded the Nobel Prize for Literature.

During the First World War, Conrad declined to join a committee, led by Sienkiewicz and Paderewski, to aid Polish war victims (he said 'I cannot join a committee where I understand Russian names will appear');[34] so no contact was established between the two writers. Nevertheless, in at least two respects Sienkiewicz's career has a bearing on Conrad's. First, the reviewer in *Blackwood's*, by alerting British readers to the importance of Polish work, was thereby helping to make *Blackwood's* potentially more receptive to the fiction which Conrad would within a few years submit to the magazine. Secondly, there was the incentive and challenge provided for Conrad by the critical acclaim and commercial success gained by a fellow-Pole. His somewhat envious view of Henryk Sienkiewicz's popularity is indicated by a letter of 1903 to a Polish friend in which he says, 'The heroic gospel of St. Henry, dear sir, reigns over the entire earth'.[35] Though Conrad eventually declined numerous literary honours (several degrees, the Order of Merit and a knighthood), he nursed keen though unfulfilled hopes of emulating Sienkiewicz by winning the Nobel Prize.

Conrad's 'Amy Foster' (1901), a melancholy story of a homesick emigrant, may be partly indebted to Sienkiewicz's 'Za chlebem' ('After Bread', 1880), the best known of several Polish tales which offered warnings of the perils of homesickness and disillusionment encountered by the peasant-exile from Poland. Conrad's Yanko Goorall, the hero of 'Amy Foster', is persuaded to leave his homeland by Austrian agents working in connivance with local Jews; he voyages from Hamburg, is shipwrecked off the English coast, suffers tribulations on land, and eventually, deserted and misunderstood, dies of a feverish illness. In Sienkiewicz's tale the agents are Germans, again conniving with Jews; the peasant-hero suffers hardship by sea and land; like Yanko, he suffers bitter pangs of homesickness and dies tragically of fever.[36]

Stefan Żeromski

In 1922 one of the leading Polish authors, Stefan Żeromski, wrote a laudatory preface to a translation of *Almayer's Folly*. Conrad sent thanks for this appreciation by 'the greatest master of [Polish] literature'.[37] Conrad had another reason for gratitude to this master. As Polish critics have pointed out,[38] Conrad's *Victory* (1915) derives some elements from Żeromski's melodramatic novel *Dzieje grzechu* (*The Story of a Sin*). The feline Ricardo and the seemingly-homosexual Mr Jones have resemblances to the tiger-like Pochroń and the seemingly-homosexual Płaza-Spławski, and in both novels a 'fallen woman' dies self-sacrificially and joyously for the man she loves. Żeromski describes thus the moment of death:

> Her whole being lit with her earliest girlish smile of happiness and with that smile of divine bliss on her lips she died, seeking his glance in the shades of death.[39]

Conrad gives:

> The flush of rapture flooding her whole being broke out in a smile of innocent, girlish happiness; and with that divine radiance on her lips she breathed her last, triumphant, seeking for his glance in the shades of death.[40]

Conrad does seem to be echoing Żeromski's phrasing, though in both cases the writing appears hackneyed and conventional. One curious aspect of this matter is that Conrad told Garnett in 1921 that he deemed *Dzieje grzechu* 'disagreeable' and unworthy of translation into English;[41] another is that in 1923, when Conrad gave a public reading in America, the passage he chose was the very section of *Victory* describing the heroine's death; and another is that in the 'Author's Note' to the novel, Conrad claims that Ricardo, Mr Jones and Lena were all suggested by real-life encounters during his travels. What is unquestionable is that in the second half of *Victory*, as the 'Żeromskian' material becomes noticeable, a potentially subtle account of an inhibited love-relationship gives way to conventional melodrama.[42]

3.2 FRENCH LITERATURE

In correspondence with British acquaintances, Conrad sometimes used the French language when offering courteous gallantries, or when expressing highly sceptical or cynical ideas ('la société est essentielment [sic] criminelle' – society is essentially criminal),[43] or when expressing some of his positive moral convictions – as in a letter to Sir Sidney Colvin in 1917:

> The humorous, the pathetic, the passionate, the sentimental *aspects* come in of themselves – mais en vérité c'est les valeurs idéales des faits et gestes humains qui se sont imposés à mon activité artistique. [But truly my artistic activity has been governed by the ideal values of human deeds and actions.][44]

Conrad, though not always accurate in it, was so fluent in French that he sometimes unthinkingly used Gallic words and idioms as if they were English. In *The Nigger of the 'Narcissus'*, for example, a heap of nails is described as 'more inabordable than a hedgehog' ('inabordable' is French for 'unapproachable'); and in *Lord Jim*, a patient 'held the doctor for an ass'.[45] One of the parody-inviting features of 'Conradese' in his early novels and tales is the frequency with which adjectives or adjectival phrases are arranged in pairs and triplets after the noun; for example: '[T]he sea, blue and profound, remained still, without a stir, without a ripple, without a wrinkle – viscous, stagnant, dead';[46] and this stylistic habit may well derive from his reading of French fiction and poetry. As Jocelyn Baines has suggested, Conrad's over-fondness for polysyllabic privative adjectives ('inconceivable', 'inscrutable', 'impenetrable', etc.) was possibly encouraged by the inflated phraseology of Pierre Loti.[47]

Of the French authors, it was probably Gustave Flaubert, however, who exerted the greatest influence on Conrad. Flaubert set the standard of extreme literary dedication: for him, literature was the central concern of life, and the great writer was one who was prepared to sacrifice all other concerns in order to construct his fictional worlds laboriously, phrase by phrase, with intense concentration and concern for *le mot juste*. Conrad's attitudes to his own art form a protean cluster, but that cluster includes a sense of Flaubertian dedication, an obsessive concern with literary truth and an avowed contempt for those who would sacrifice literature on the altar of commerce. During anguished struggles, Conrad would sometimes compare himself with Mâtho (in Flaubert's *Salammbô*) who, though tortured and mutilated, 'marchait toujours' – defiantly maintained his progress.[48] Significantly, Flaubert's strengths as a writer were much in his mind at the very beginning of his literary career, for, in a letter of 1892, while he was slowly building *Almayer's Folly*, Conrad wrote to Marguerite Poradowska:

> [Y]ou remind me a little of Flaubert, whose *Madame Bovary* I have just reread with respectful admiration. . . . . In him, we see a man who had enough imagination for two realists. There are few authors who could be as much a creator as he. One never questions for a moment either his characters or his incidents; one would rather doubt one's own existence.[49]

Flaubert had striven for cool lucidity in depicting life as it is, warts and all; he brought a new scrupulous diligence of attention to ostensibly mediocre lives in mediocre settings; and though he scandalised some of his earlier readers (he was prosecuted for offending public morality) and gave an impression of life-denying aestheticism to many subsequent readers, not only a new honesty but also a new kind of human poignancy emerges from his apparently ruthless observations. Certainly Flaubert would have strengthened Conrad's preoccupation, so evident in *Almayer's Folly*, with blighted communication and egoistic delusion. Indeed, as Ian Watt has suggested, 'Almayer is a Borneo Bovary':

> Like Emma, he devotes his entire life to one obsessive fantasy – although not of great love but of great wealth. Both Almayer and Emma begin by making a loveless marriage merely as a step towards realising their fantasies; and then, refusing to abandon their early dreams and come to terms with the ordinariness of their own selves and of the lives offered by Sambir or Yonville, they are steadily driven into a deepening tangle of circumstances from which death is the only way out.[50]

Almayer, Willems, Lingard, Jim, Kurtz, Gould: all of them, in various ways, are impelled by dreams; and all are ambushed by recalcitrant circumstances.

By the time of 'Heart of Darkness', Conrad was to surpass his master not only in political and cultural range but also in densely evocative richness of implication. Even the short tale 'An Outpost of Progress' shows how Conrad could use, but transcend, Flaubertian material. The heroes of Flaubert's *Bouvard et Pécuchet* are well-meaning but ingenuous comrades whose schemes for improving their own condition and that of the countryside around them repeatedly result in fiasco; during a phase of disillusionment, they quarrel over two spoonfuls of tea and then make abortive preparations for suicide. Echoes of *Bouvard et Pécuchet* can be heard in 'An Outpost of Progress', in which two ingenuous comrades (Kayerts and Carlier) share schemes for improving their condition and that of the African countryside around them; demoralised by isolation, they quarrel over a lump of sugar; Kayerts shoots his comrade and hangs himself. The Flaubertian echoes, however, draw attention to the enormous contrast between the two texts. *Bouvard et Pécuchet* is long, diffuse, repetitive and unfinished; it seems longer than it is, because Flaubert persists in repeating the point which had been emphatically made in the first two chapters – that the comrades' theories and experiments are doomed to failure, and that the only gainers will be the astute peasants and bourgeoisie of Normandy. Conrad's brief tale, on the other hand, is a masterpiece of compression: in a few pages it conveys, both by aloofly sceptical commentary and by ferociously ironic images, the absurdity and hypocrisy of the 'imperial mission' in Africa.

Another French author admired by Conrad was Guy de Maupassant, the prolific writer of urbane novels and drily ironic tales. Conrad claimed to be 'saturated by Maupassant';[51] when established in his literary career, he provided an introduction to a selection of Maupassant's stories; and various debts have been documented by scholars. The Heyst–Lena relationship in *Victory* is partly foreshadowed in Maupassant's *Fort comme le mort*; the celebrated Preface to *The Nigger of the 'Narcissus'* echoes some of the phrases of Maupassant's Preface to *Pierre et Jean*, while *The Nigger* itself derives occasional descriptive touches from the novel *Bel-Ami*.[52] When Forestier of *Bel-Ami* is dying, his hands move restlessly over the bed-sheets, his breathing seems too rapid to be counted and so weak as to be scarcely audible; he has a terrified vision of death, crying 'The cemetery ... I ... my God!'; as he expires, his eyes close 'like two lamps which are extinguished', and two threads of blood appear at the corners of his mouth. The description of James Wait's death in *The Nigger* incorporates similar or identical details, and the phrasing is too close to be explained as coincidence. Even the ship's cat in Conrad's novel copies the posture of the cat in *Bel-Ami*: both relax 'in the pose of a crouching chimera'.[53] As a whole, *The Nigger of the 'Narcissus'*, the narrative of a sea-voyage, is quite unlike *Bel-Ami*, the study of a cynical careerist in Parisian society; but the debts to Maupassant exemplify a general rule of Conradian fiction: that even those tales and novels which seem to be distinctively based on Conrad's own past experiences may be embellished by vivid details seized with a magpie's adroitness from other writers' novels, tales or memoirs.

'A Smile of Fortune', for example, seems to be strongly autobiographical in its account of a sea-captain's infatuation with a sheltered young woman on the island of Mauritius; and there is sound biographical evidence that when Conrad visited Mauritius in 1888 as captain of the *Otago*, he courted a woman who, to his dismay, proved to be already betrothed.[54] Yet Conrad's tale repeatedly echoes Maupassant's 'Les Soeurs Rondoli'. For instance, Maupassant tells how, on a journey through Provence to the Mediterranean, the air becomes rich with the smell of roses and orange-groves; when Conrad's hero visits the heroine, she is seated in a walled garden lush with flowers which fill the air with their heavy scent. More strikingly, Alice in 'A Smile of Fortune' resembles a reincarnation of Francesca in 'Les Soeurs Rondoli'. Both heroines are seductive yet slatternly; taciturn, brusque and nonchalant. Francesca often repeats 'Che mi ta' ('What does it matter to me?' and 'Mica' ('Not at all'); and the narrator mocks this trait: 'Je ne vous appellerai plus que Mlle Mica' ('I shall simply call you Miss Not at all'). Alice, similarly, repeats 'Won't!', 'Shan't!' and 'Don't care!', and the narrator remarks: '[S]ometimes I would address her as Miss "Don't Care"'. Both heroines have a mass of rich black hair, somewhat untidy and giving an impression of a heavy weight. Francesca has

> black hair, wavy, slightly frizzly; so dense, vigorous and long that it seemed heavy, so that merely to look at it gave you the sensation of its weight on the head. . . . .[55]

And Alice's hair is

> a mass of black, lustrous locks, twisted anyhow high on her head, with long, untidy wisps hanging down on each side of the clear sallow face; a mass so thick and strong and abundant that, nothing but to look at, it gave you a sensation of heavy pressure on the top of your head. . . . .[56]

('Nothing but to look at' is evidently Conrad's un-idiomatic translation of the original phrase, 'rien qu'à les voir'). Furthermore, as Paul Kirschner has pointed out,[57] even a classically Conradian reflection on the emptiness of life proves to be a near-translation from Maupassant. The narrator of 'Les Soeurs Rondoli' says:

> It is by travelling far that one well understands how everything is common, short and empty; it is in seeking the unknown that one clearly perceives how everything is mediocre and soon ended. . . . .[58]

Conrad's captain reflects:

> [T]he further one ventures the better one understands how
> everything in our life is common, short and empty; . . . . . it is in
> seeking the unknown in our sensations that we discover how
> mediocre are our attempts and how soon defeated![59]

Maupassant was not the only French author from whom Conrad
derived the phrasing of attitudes which seem distinctively
Conradian. In two book-reviews (in *The Speaker* for 16 July 1904
and in *The English Review* for December 1908), Conrad paid tribute
to the 'princely' genius, the sceptical humanity, of Anatole France.
From the pages of France, Conrad derived not only reinforcement
of his own bleak view of history and human nature but also (as
Owen Knowles has shown)[60] instances of lucidly epigrammatic
phrasing. In the essay 'Mérimée', for example, France sums up as
follows the character of the novelist Prosper Mérimée:

> What should he regret? He had never recognised anything but
> energy as virtue or anything but passions as duties. Was not his
> sadness rather that of the sceptic for whom the universe is only
> a succession of incomprehensible images. . . . . ?[61]

And years later, in *Nostromo*, Conrad sums up as follows the
character of Decoud:

> What should he regret? He had recognised no other virtue than
> intelligence, and had erected passions into duties. . . . . His
> sadness was the sadness of a sceptical mind. He beheld the
> universe as a succession of incomprehensible images.[62]

As Shakespeare took ideas and phrases from Plutarch and
Holinshed, seizing and re-animating, so Conrad used his French
mentors. In his Polish reading, characteristic tones were those of
romantic idealism and lyrical affirmation; the French writers provided contrasting tones – urbane scepticism, cool delineation of
the sensuous and mundane. Both helped to establish the characteristic paradoxical richness of mature Conradian fiction, which is
both lyrical and sceptical, both romantic and ironic; capable of
majestically Olympian generalisation and of minutely sharp description.

3.3 ENGLISH LITERATURE

Conrad read voraciously among classic and non-classic English texts: some indication of the range is provided by his works' epigraphs, which include citations of Chaucer, Spenser, Shakespeare, Sir Thomas Browne, Samuel Pepys, Keats and Arthur Symons. Chaucer's 'Franklin's Tale' provided the epigraph for *The Rescue*, and those three quoted lines invoke a tale of trust and generosity which provides a potent and bitterly ironic counterpoint to Conrad's narrative of incommunication, frustration and betrayal. The Spenserian epigraph to *The Rover* ('Sleep after toyle, port after stormie seas, / Ease after warre, death after life, does greatly please') seems, out of its context in *The Faerie Queene*, to be finely appropriate to the character of old Peyrol who, in *The Rover*, is making his preparations for death and chooses a heroically suicidal end; and eventually the Spenserian quotation was inscribed on Conrad's grave-stone at Canterbury. For both these uses of the quotation, however, a knowledge of the literary context is counter-productive and indeed embarrassing, since the speaker of those words in *The Faerie Queene* is 'a man of hell, that cals himselfe *Despaire*',[63] and who, by his praise of death, seeks to lure the unwary to suicide and damnation. Sometimes, then, an epigraph implies Conrad's knowledge of the context and invites the reader to apply both the quoted phrases and their context to the Conradian novel or tale, while at other times it seems to have been chosen in a more casual way for its immediate thematic associations.

One of the best instances of Conrad's ability to blend literary source-materials with autobiographical reminiscence is provided by *The Shadow-Line*. In its locations and itinerary, in some of its characterisations and situations, it clearly draws on Conrad's memory of his first voyage as captain of the *Otago*, a slow voyage from Bangkok to Singapore. The epigraph from Baudelaire's 'La Musique' ('D'autres fois, calme plat, grand miroir / De mon désespoir') has obvious thematic relevance to the plight of the young captain, reduced almost to mental breakdown by the purgatorial voyage. The hero, introspective and fearful of proving inadequate to the task which chance has presented to him, has some Hamlet-like characteristics (chief of them being a habit of unavailing self-reproach), and appropriately the text contains several echoes of Shakespeare's *Hamlet*: 'this stale, unprofitable

world of my discontent', 'an undiscovered country', 'that force
somewhere within our lives which shapes them this way or that',
'unknown powers that shape our destinies', and 'the mortal
coil'.[64] A particularly strong literary influence appears to be
Coleridge's 'Rime of the Ancyent Marinere'. In both that poem
and *The Shadow-Line*, an accursed ship is a place of torment for the
narrator. In the poem, the mariner bears a burden of guilt and
feels that he is subject to reproachful gazes from the crew; so
does the young captain in the novel. Both works evoke superbly
the tedium and torpor when a ship is long becalmed in warm
seas. At the climax of the poem, there comes a sudden rain and
wind, and the dead crew, rising as spectres, begin to haul on the
ropes; and at the climax of the novel, there comes a sudden rain
and wind, and the crew – virtually all of whom have been very ill
– man the ropes like ghosts:

> Those men were the ghosts of themselves, and their weight on
> a rope could be no more than the weight of a bunch of ghosts.[65]

Nevertheless, Conrad and Coleridge were able to draw on a
traditional fund of legends of the sea, a tradition as old as Jonah
and which culminates in the legend of the Flying Dutchman; and
Conrad makes explicit allusion to the Flying Dutchman both in
The Shadow-Line and in 'Falk'.[66]

Among novelists, it is probable that the Englishman whose
work Conrad most enjoyed was Charles Dickens. As a boy, he
had read *Nicholas Nickleby* ('It is extraordinary how well Mrs.
Nickleby could chatter disconnectedly in Polish');[67] and Conrad's
letters, reminiscences and fictional works are peppered with
Dickensian references. In *Chance*, the narrator notes that once de
Barral had clung to his child beside his wife's grave and later
walked hand in hand with his daughter at the seaside, and
comments: 'Pictures from Dickens – pregnant with pathos.'[68] In *A
Personal Record*, Conrad remarks that a forbidding acquaintance of
his Marseille days, Madame Delestang, reminded him of Lady
Dedlock in *Bleak House*.[69] And in 'Poland Revisited' he recalls his
first visit to a shipping office in London:

> A Dickensian nook of London, that wonder city, the growth of
> which bears no sign of intelligent design, but many traces of
> freakishly sombre phantasy the Great Master knew so well how

to bring out by the magic of his understanding love. And the office I entered was Dickensian too. The dust of the Waterloo year lay on the panes and frames of its windows. . . . .[70]

'Freakishly sombre phantasy': the similarity between the two writers lies mainly in their powers of creation of grotesquerie. In *The Secret Agent* particularly, Conrad makes London a theatre of savage farce by using the Dickensian technique of investing the inanimate with an unexpected degree of life (a pianola plays spontaneously, houses have apparently strayed from their correct locations) while investing the animate – the men and women – with an alarming degree of automatism. Again, there is a rather Dickensian quality about Conrad's atmospheric rendering of London in that novel: to live there is like living at the bottom of a filthy, muddy and stagnant aquarium; so that the slimy London of *Bleak House* comes to mind. In both cases the murk seems to be a moral murk and not simply a meteorological misfortune. Stevie, the hapless innocent who is destroyed after summing up his wisdom in the maxim 'Bad world for poor people', seems to be a relative of Dickens' bewildered Jo; while Detective-Inspector Heat is a stalwart descendant of Dickens' Inspector Bucket; and both Conrad and Dickens knew the ancient aphorism ('Truth lies at the bottom of a deep well') which generated Bucket's symbolic surname.[71] The scene in which Winnie Verloc's bewigged mother crosses the city in a rattling cab drawn by an emaciated horse approaches a Dickensian vividness of farce, fantasy and the grimly macabre. It is still not a *very* close approach: there are important differences between the two men. Dickens has a rich creative exuberance, an eruptive fecundity of comic and absurd invention, which the more austere and laborious Conrad lacks; and Conrad has a more mature control of the elements of his works than the relatively manic and opportunistic Dickens possesses.

Both Charles Dickens and Dickens' admirer, Thomas Carlyle (whose *Sartor Resartus* Conrad knew),[72] provide British precedent for some aspects of Conrad's political radicalism. Dickens and Carlyle are fervently eloquent when exposing and denouncing the injustice and brutality of industrialism in the nineteenth century; yet their attack proceeds not from socialist premises but from 'organicist conservative' premises: they seek a hierarchic society in which the concept of *noblesse oblige* guides the high, while grateful deference guides the low – an attempt to convert industrial society into an idealised harmonious feudal state. And certainly, in *The Nigger of the 'Narcissus'*, Conrad came close to recommending that 'feudal' pattern of society: a corporate, hierarchic and authoritarian community. By the time of *Nostromo*, however, Conrad's increasing sense of the inevitability of class conflict had helped him to outgrow that model.

3.4 A NOTE ON PHILOSOPHICAL AND SCIENTIFIC MATTERS

Conrad responded so fully to the main currents of philosophical thought and to the scientific debates of his day that several volumes could be devoted to their influence on his works. Here I note briefly some of the main factors.

A distinctive feature of Conrad's early and mature writings from *Almayer's Folly* to *Nostromo* is his tendency to refer to facts, beliefs and opinions (and even feelings of love) as 'illusions'. (Max Beerbohm's parody of Conrad was to give gleefully close attention to this feature.)[73] Although such scepticism derives in part from Conrad's reading of Maupassant and Anatole France, an important influence was Schopenhauer's *Die Welt als Wille und Vorstellung* (*The World as Will and Idea*). Galsworthy reports that Conrad studied Schopenhauer,[74] and certainly the 'Author's Note' to *The Nigger* echoes some of the views of art given in *The World as Will and Idea*.[75] More obviously, in *Victory* the opinions of Heyst's father seem to be modelled on Schopenhauer's dismally pessimistic aphorisms.[76] Characteristically, Conrad puts the life-denying ideas in a largely critical context: Heyst dies after making an affirmation of life and love which contradicts his father's philosophy, even though the workings of the plot may appear to endorse the view that one should seek detachment from the blandishments of the world. This ability to use ideas in a paradoxical mode of partial endorsement and partial criticism is illustrated by the Darwinian themes of 'Heart of Darkness'. While that tale strongly evokes the themes of *The Origin of Species*, it ruthlessly denies the optimistic gloss which, in the conclusion of that work, Darwin placed on his own findings.[77] Similarly, *The Secret Agent* both exploits and mocks the purportedly scientific theories of Cesare Lombroso, author of volumes on criminal anthropology:

there the disciple of Lombroso's theories, Comrade Ossipon, is unable to perceive that he himself could serve as a grotesque illustration in one of his master's books on physically-identifiable criminality and degeneracy.[78]

Early reviewers sometimes classified Conrad as a literary 'naturalist'.[79] Although 'naturalism' is often used loosely as a synonym for 'realism', a stricter usage defines it as the school of writing whose doyens include Zola and Strindberg, characterised by the writer's determination to provide a supposedly scientific (particularly Darwinian) warrant for human actions. Conrad's tale 'Falk' has a naturalistic edge when it suggests that just as a gourmet's delight in an exquisite meal is a sophistication of a savage's glee at a cannibalistic orgy, so 'the infinite gradation in shades and in flavour of our discriminating love' is an evolutionary refinement of a predatory sexual appetite.[80] In *The Secret Agent*, a particularly 'Zolaesque' passage occurs when Winnie Verloc stabs her husband:

Into that plunging blow ..... Mrs. Verloc had put all the inheritance of her immemorial and obscure descent, the simple ferocity of the age of caverns, and the unbalanced nervous fury of the age of bar-rooms.[81]

A recurrent feature of Conrad's work is the distinctive symbolic power given to imagery of darkness: the nightscapes in 'Heart of Darkness', *Nostromo* and *The Shadow-Line* carry suggestions of the mortality not only of the individual but also of the human race itself. For Victorians the popularisation of Lord Kelvin's second law of thermodynamics (the law of the entropy of available energy) had created the nightmarish vista of a future in which the sun would cool in the sky and all life would perish on a dying, darkening earth. In the essay 'Henry James', at least, Conrad postulated that even on that last day, an artist will be present to tell its story:

The artist in his calling of interpreter creates (the clearest form of demonstration) because he must. He is so much of a voice that, for him, silence is like death; and the postulate was, that there is a group alive, clustered on his threshold to watch the last flicker of light on a black sky, to hear the last word uttered in the stilled workshop of the earth.[82]

4
Phases in Conrad's Literary Development

Various people helped Conrad to complete *Almayer's Folly*. One was Marguerite Poradowska, to whom he sent bulletins on the progress of the manuscript, and who evidently provided encouraging comments and requests for further glimpses of the unfolding narrative. Other helpers were Ted Sanderson (a schoolmaster whom Conrad had met on the *Torrens* in 1893) and Ted's mother. Conrad took the manuscript to the schoolhouse at Elstree; and Mrs Reynolds (sister of John Galsworthy, who had accompanied Sanderson on the *Torrens* voyage) noted that both the Sandersons

> took a hand, and considerable trouble, in editing the already amazingly excellent English of their Polish friend's 'Almayer' manuscript, and in generally screwing up Conrad's courage to the sticking-point of publication.[1]

Although he reported to Marguerite Poradowska on 24 April 1894 that Almayer had died and the book was finished, Conrad continued to revise it; among other things, he re-wrote parts of Chapter 1 so as to emphasise Almayer's love for his daughter.[2]

Conrad next decided to send the manuscript to Edmund Gosse, the distinguished critic, for advice. As Jocelyn Baines notes, Gosse was at that time editing for Heinemann an 'International Library' of foreign novels translated into English: 'perhaps Conrad thought that a novel in English by a Pole might fit into the series'.[3]

Although there is no corroborative evidence of Gosse's participation in the matter, it seems possible that it was Gosse who advised Conrad to submit the manuscript to Fisher Unwin as a candidate for Unwin's 'Pseudonym Library'. Conrad chose the pseudonym 'Kamudi' (Malay for 'rudder') and entered it on the title-page. The manuscript remained at the publishers for some weeks without response; Conrad became impatient, and suggested to Marguerite Poradowska that he should retrieve it and send it to her: she could then translate it into French and seek a continental publisher. Conrad even suggested that her name should appear on the title-page 'with merely an explanatory note to say that K. collaborated in the book'.[4] A variant of this scheme was that the novel, translated by Marguerite, should be offered for serialisation in *Revue des Deux Mondes*. In the meantime, Conrad began work on his second novel. Even before the fate of the first was known, he was busy with its successor.

At Fisher Unwin's, *Almayer's Folly* was read by W. H. Chesson, who described himself as 'Mr. Unwin's receiver and weeder of MSS'. 'The magical melancholy of that masterpiece submerged me', he recalled.[5] The manuscript was also seen by Edward Garnett, who commented, 'Hold on to this'.[6] Accordingly, Chesson submitted to his employer a favourable report and, at an interview with Conrad, Fisher Unwin offered the author a choice: either payment of £20 and no royalties, or a share of any profits if the author would agree to contribute to the cost of publication. Conrad chose the former option, while reserving French translation rights. The novel would appear under his own name, having proved too long for entry in the Pseudonym Library (for which the maximum limit was 36 000 words). Fisher Unwin – on whom Conrad and Garnett subsequently conferred the sarcastic title of 'Enlightened Patron of Letters' – drove hard bargains: he employed Garnett at the paltry wage of ten shillings per week, and when he published John Galsworthy's first volume in 1897 (a collection of short stories in an edition of 500 copies) the author paid the costs of publication.[7] As the publisher explained to Conrad, there were obvious risks with *Almayer's Folly*: the novel might be good, but its author was unknown and the story might not please the public's taste; on the other hand, the author could be assured that his book would appear in a handsome six-shilling volume which would be guaranteed long notices in two prestigious magazines, the *Saturday Review* and the *Athenaeum*,[8] in addition to receiving widespread attention in the press. (These were accurate assurances: *Almayer's Folly* did indeed receive full and widespread critical attention.) In the meantime, suggested Fisher Unwin, Conrad should write a similar but shorter novel as a candidate for the Pseudonym Library.

T. Fisher Unwin has himself received a rather bad press over the years as a cold, calculating, tightfisted publisher. In fairness, then, it should be noted that when, in 1894, Chesson and Garnett perceived at once the merit of Conrad's first work, he acted without demur on Chesson's recommendation, met the author personally, encouraged him to maintain his literary ambitions, provided exceptional publicity,[9] and entered into a detailed postal discussion of Conrad's future works. ('He has *means* to push a book – the connection and the best agent in the trade', the author observed.)[10] Conrad, temperamentally prickly yet depressively self-doubting, needed such encouragement even more than would most novitiates. While *Almayer's Folly* was proceeding into print, both Chesson and Garnett entered into friendly correspondence with their new author. Chesson, who had the task of drafting advertisements for the novel, consulted Conrad, who suggested: 'Could you not say something about being a "civilized story in savage surroundings?" Something in that sense if not in those words. . . . .' (Chesson readily complied.)[11] Conrad's friendship with Garnett, though strained by the latter's anarchistic sympathies and advocacy of Russian novelists, was to endure for life; and, without doubt, Garnett's critical acuity influenced numerous works by his friend. As late as 1920, when converting the serial of *The Rescue* into the book, Conrad reported: 'all your remarks and suggestions . . . . . have been adopted and followed except in one instance'.[12]

Edward Garnett (1868–1937) worked as a publisher's reader first for Fisher Unwin, then for Heinemann, and subsequently for Gerald Duckworth (on a salary of just £15 per month) until the First World War, when he served in the Friends' Ambulance Corps in Italy. After the war he worked for John Lane and finally for Jonathan Cape, who had been sales manager at Duckworth's. Garnett would call at the publisher's office to return manuscripts with his reports, would collect a fresh batch of manuscripts and return either to his London base, 19 Pond Place, Chelsea, or to his cottage, the Cearne, on the Kent–Sussex border. C. G. Heilbrun remarks:

The Cearne was, in its isolation, symbolic of Edward's attitude toward the world. He and Constance chose to build their small house in a hidden pasture. The Cearne – so named because it was encearned (encircled) by forest – stood half a mile from any road, approachable only by cart-track through the woods. Mr David Garnett says his parents' choice of site reflected their awareness that they did not fit into the Victorian social hierarchy, and did not wish to belong to a community.[13]

His guests at the Cearne were to include Conrad, Ford Madox Hueffer (later to be known as Ford Madox Ford), W. H. Hudson, Stephen Crane, John Galsworthy, Edward Thomas and D. H. Lawrence: 'They had been recognized by Edward, not yet by the world.'[14] In London, he inaugurated a long series of Tuesday luncheons at the Mont Blanc Restaurant in Gerrard Street, Soho: occasions which served as a meeting place and debating chamber for Hudson and Norman Douglas, joined occasionally by Edward Thomas, D. M. Tomlinson, John Masefield, Galsworthy, Belloc and Cunninghame Graham. After D. H. Lawrence's death, Frieda Lawrence told Edward:

[W]e neither of us forgot, ever what you meant to us in our first being together or what you meant to Lawrence as the midwife of his genius![15]

'Midwife of genius' might indeed epitomise Edward Garnett's activities. He not only read manuscripts with an exceptionally sharp eye for imaginative originality and distinction; he also strove to get those manuscripts into print; he would meet and correspond with their authors, encouraging, cajoling, criticising; he would urge them to read works which he felt might provide artistic challenge and sustenance, would introduce his favourite writers to others, and could influentially review their publications in periodicals like the *Speaker*, the *Academy* or the *Nation*. ('The ruck takes its tone from you', Conrad told him.)[16] Though 'poor as a church mouse',[17] he sometimes lent money to authors who, like D. H. Lawrence, were slow to repay.

It can be argued that when the cultural climate needs to be changed, most literary critics and reviewers are peripheral, for they assess texts which are *already* in print; whereas astute readers like Garnett are central, for they decide which texts are worthy to appear in print. Writers whose careers were established largely through the endeavours of Garnett included Galsworthy, W. H. Hudson, Cunninghame Graham, W. H. Davies, D. H. Lawrence, Dorothy Richardson, T. E. Lawrence, H. E. Bates and Henry Green. Green said of him:

> Like a St Bernard he could smell out the half-frozen body which, if encouraged, might yet be able to wrestle with words. The bottle of brandy hung round his neck was flattery, and at the next meeting with him it was blame. Afterwards he bullied you with a mixture of blame–flattery, nearly always to your good.[18]

In *The Inheritors*, the novel written jointly by Conrad and Ford (1901), Fisher Unwin was to appear as the miserly Polehampton, while Garnett was to be affectionately commemorated as Lea:

> Lea had helped me a good deal in the old days – he had helped everybody, for that matter. You would probably find traces of Lea's influence in the beginnings of every writer of about my decade; of everybody who ever did anything decent, and of some who never got beyond the stage of burgeoning decently. He had given me the material help that a publisher's reader could give, until his professional reputation was endangered, and he had given me the more valuable help that so few can give. . . . .
> He was sprawling angularly on a cane lounge, surrounded by whole heaps of manuscript. . . . .
> And on the floor, on the chairs, on the sideboard, on the unmade bed, the profusion of manuscripts.[19]

Garnett's letters to Conrad and Cunninghame Graham in the 1890s make clear his tastes and predilections. He disliked conservative, flabby, sentimental, cliché-bound writing, and advocated radicalism, irony, scepticism, vivid imagery and a romanticism controlled by closely realistic observation. In July 1896, when Conrad completed one of his most ruthlessly ironic and sceptical tales, 'An Outpost of Progress', he wrote to Garnett:

> I send it to you first of all. It's yours. It shall be the first of a vol ded[icated] to you – but this story is *meant* for you. I am pleased

with it. That's why you shall get it. . . . . If any passages are – de trop – then strike out.[20]

Garnett recalled that when (as a twenty-six-year-old) he had first read the manuscript of *Almayer's Folly*, he became eager to meet its author:

> What particularly captivated me in the novel was the figure of Babalatchi, the aged one-eyed statesman, and the night scene at the river's edge between Mrs. Almayer and her daughter. The strangeness of the tropical atmosphere, and the poetic 'realism' of this romantic narrative excited my curiosity about the author, who I fancied might have eastern blood in his veins.

And, at the subsequent meeting, this was his impression of Conrad:

> My memory is of seeing a dark-haired man, short but extremely graceful in his nervous gestures, with brilliant eyes, now narrowed and penetrating, now soft and warm, with a manner alert yet caressing, whose speech was ingratiating, guarded, and brusque turn by turn. I had never seen before a man so masculinely keen yet so femininely sensitive.[21]

Conrad, who characteristically responded to friendly overtures with seductively ingratiating flattery, subsequently suggested that without Garnett's encouragement he might not have proceeded to write his second and successive novels. As we have seen, Conrad had actually commenced his second novel even before the first was accepted by a publisher. It is certainly the case, however, that Conrad showed parts of *An Outcast of the Islands* to Garnett as he completed them, solicited and studied Garnett's comments, and sometimes excised passages on the young reader's advice: 'All the paragraphs marked by You to that effect shall be cut out'.[22] At Conrad's flat in Gillingham Street (behind Victoria Station), Garnett had emphasised 'the necessity for a writer to follow his own path and disregard the public's taste'; his host, however, retorted: 'But I *won't* live in an attic! . . . . . I'm past that, you understand? I *won't* live in an attic!'[23] That exchange sets the keynote for the bitterness and agonies of Conrad's subsequent years as a writer: on the one hand, Conrad valued the highest

standards of literary integrity; on the other, he needed to earn a
living by pleasing the public; and his writings were to veer
between acute subtlety and melodramatic banality as he responded to the resultant tension.

Almayer's Folly was published, in the six-shilling edition that
Fisher Unwin had promised, on 29 April 1895. Even before that
date, favourable publicity had appeared (evidently arranged by
W. H. Chesson): on 25 April, the *Daily News* announced:

> No novelist has yet annexed the island of Borneo – in itself
> almost a continent. But Mr. Joseph Conrad, a new writer, is
> about to make the attempt in a novel entitled *Almayer's Folly*,
> which Mr. Unwin will publish. Mr. Conrad says that he com-
> bines 'the psychological study of a sensitive European living
> alone among semi-hostile Arabs and Malays with the vivid
> incidents attaching to the life of pirates and smugglers.' A
> merely 'sensitive' European has no business among the semi-
> savages of Borneo. What you want is an unbounded, reckless
> hospitality to all sorts of impressions. However the story is
> praised by those who have seen it in manuscript. The author is
> intimately acquainted with Borneo and its people. The physical
> setting of his story is as picturesque as the world offers. The
> European's closest friend is an ex-pirate, and the reassertion of
> the old savage instinct in the pirate's lovely daughter – an
> atavistic fit, if that be not too rude an expression – is one of the
> chief incidents of the tale.[24]

This 'kite' or 'trailer' for the book says a good deal about marketing
tactics. In the first place, one reason for the appearance of this
item in that paper is that Fisher Unwin advertised regularly in the
Liberal *Daily News*. Next, the paragraph opens with a candid
acknowledgement of the inter-relationship between political and
literary imperialism: a new act of annexation is to take place – this
time, the literary annexation of Borneo. The statement attributed
to Conrad looks like an expansion of his remark to Chesson
('Could you not say something about being a "civilized story in
savage surroundings?"') and artfully appeals both to intellectuals
('the psychological study of a sensitive European') and to readers
seeking a lively yarn ('vivid incidents . . . . pirates and smugglers').
The columnist's misgiving ('What you want is an unbounded,
reckless hospitality to all sorts of impressions') shows how, at this

time, the words 'impressions' and 'impressionism' were becoming
stock critical terms: the French Impressionist painters had gained
respectability and acclaim by the 1890s, and writers now frequently
sought to inherit the mantle of 'impressionism'. As for the paragraph's final remark on 'the reassertion of the old savage instinct
in the pirate's lovely daughter' (which confuses Nina Almayer
with Lingard's protégé): this clearly offers a blandishment to
readers hoping for sexual titillation coupled with a little racial
voyeurism.

Most of the features specified in this publicity-notice are
certainly to be found in Conrad's novel. A remarkable aspect of
many of Conrad's novels and tales is that, in brief and superficial
summary, they seem to belong to the realm of popular commercial
fiction. *Almayer's Folly* does indeed tell of piracy, smuggling,
shipwreck, exotic races, strife in the jungle, and the elopement of
a beautiful Eurasian with a Balinese prince. But Conrad made
adventure introspective, heroism ambiguous, the exotic subvers-
ive; he liked to undermine stereotypical contrasts between the
'civilised' and the 'primitive'; and dominant themes in *Almayer's
Folly* include the isolation of individuals and the littleness of
humanity beside the inhuman vastness of nature. He transmuted
the elements of romantic melodrama into the ambiguities of
philosophical tragedy. His first novel is in some ways cumbrous
and laboured, with its strenuously wrought and sometimes over-
wrought descriptive set-pieces; it lacks the incisive verve and
impressionistic variety of his mature works. Yet it remains formidable in its philosophical and political pessimism, in its modula-
tions from lyrical melancholy to macabre black comedy, and in its
justified obliquities in narrative technique. One of those obliquities
is the use of 'delayed decoding',[25] whereby the reader is presented
with an effect but is denied (for a while at least) the understanding
of its cause; and a related obliquity is the use of the 'covert plot'.[26]
The main covert plot of *Almayer's Folly* is Abdulla's scheme to
destroy Almayer, his trade rival, by betraying Dain to the Dutch
authorities; as a consequence of the betrayal, Dain's elopement to
Bali with Nina Almayer is precipitated, Almayer's hopes of finding
gold and returning to Europe with his beloved daughter are
dashed, and Almayer's drug-stupefied death ensues. And appropriately the novel ends with a sanctimonious prayer from Abdulla
over the body of 'this Infidel he had fought so long and bested so
many times'. What makes this plot covert is that for most of the

time the reader shares the viewpoint of Almayer, the half-uncomprehending victim of the scheme; only a careful subsequent reading of the text is likely to reveal the full extent to which the dynamics of events have been provided by Abdulla's intrigue. Similarly, although the novel has some recourse to racial stereotypes, not until a second reading may one fully appreciate the extent to which those stereotypical contrasts have been questioned by the sceptical emphasis on common features: dreams of power and avarice, it seems, make the whole world kin. As Conrad remarked to Edward Garnett: 'every individual wishes to assert his power, woman by sentiment, man by achievement of some sort – mostly base.'[27] He gave a more positive version of the same notion of 'common humanity' in an 'Author's Note' which was intended as a preface to *Almayer's Folly* but which, though written near the beginning of 1895, did not appear in print until 1920. In response to Alice Meynell's complaints that literature of exotic outposts was 'decivilized', Conrad argued that the differences between Europeans and distant races were only skin-deep:

> I am content to sympathize with common mortals, no matter where they live – in houses or in tents, in the streets under a fog, or in the forests behind the dark line of dismal mangroves that fringe the vast solitude of the sea. For, their land – like ours – lies under the inscrutable eyes of the Most High. Their hearts – like ours – must endure the load of the gifts from Heaven: the curse of facts and the blessing of illusions; the bitterness of our wisdom and the deceptive consolation of our folly.[28]

On its appearance in April 1895 in England (May in the United States), *Almayer's Folly* was reviewed extensively; sometimes briefly, often – with ample quotations – at considerable length. A few of the reviews were curtly hostile; several were mixed; but high praise predominated. Certainly the *World* declared the book 'wearisome' and 'dull', while the *Nation* (USA) remarked: 'Borneo is a fine field for the study of monkeys, not men.'[29] Other complaints were that the story was 'hard to follow'; 'The action drags' (*Bookman*); and that 'some of the . . . . . characters are terribly deficient in outline' (*Academy*).[30] The dominant emphasis, however, was on the emergence of a distinctive and powerful new writer. The *Scotsman* found the novel 'remarkable' and 'powerfully imagined'; the *Daily Chronicle* said: 'Mr. Conrad has

..... the art of creating an atmosphere, poetic, romantic ..... Mr. Conrad may go on, and with confidence; he will find his public, and he deserves his place'; the *Athenaeum*, while regretting the stylistic 'convolutions', emphasised the book's promise: 'We shall await with interest Mr. Conrad's next appearance as a novelist'; H. G. Wells in the *Saturday Review* said: 'It is indeed exceedingly well imagined and well written, and it will certainly secure Mr. Conrad a high place among contemporary story-tellers'; and the *Speaker* found it 'distinctly powerful', and declared: 'If Mr. Conrad can give us another story as striking and life-like as this, his place in our literature ought to be an assured one.'[31] *Literary News* and the *Spectator* added their applause, the latter remarking: 'The name of Mr. Joseph Conrad is new to us, but it appears to us as if he might become the Kipling of the Malay Archipelago.'[32] And in the *Weekly Sun*, the editor (T. P. O'Connor, who was later to serialise *Nostromo* in *T. P.'s Weekly*) devoted over seven and a half columns, including the whole front page, to this 'startling, unique, splendid book'.[33] On the whole, then, this was a body of reviews to provide Conrad not only with gratification but with very strong encouragement to become a full-time fiction-writer.

In his letters, Conrad was often to emphasise the loneliness of the ordeal of the dedicated author; sometimes he disparaged the taste of the reading public and complained at the obtuseness of various reviewers. Yet, predictably, he was impatient to see *Almayer's Folly* in print, was excited when it appeared, and avidly studied the reviews as they appeared or were transmitted to him from the publisher and from a press-clippings agency.[34] He was also gratified to tell Marguerite Poradowska on 2 May, 'The first edition of 1100 copies has been sold';[35] but here he was counting the unhatched. At Garnett's instigation, David Rice, the 'traveller' for Fisher Unwin, had indeed persuaded the booksellers to stock almost the whole edition; nevertheless, as Garnett later noted, there's a big difference between stocking and selling:

Mr. Rice tells me that the majority of the copies rested for years on the booksellers' shelves, and that the title *Almayer's Folly* long remained a jest in 'the trade' at his own expense. Conrad's first book took seven years to get into the third impression and both *The Outcast of the Islands*, which received brilliant reviews, and *Tales of Unrest*, took each eleven years to reach a second impression. Even worse, relatively, was the case of *The Nigger of* the *'Narcissus'* (1897) which in spite of a general blast of eulogy from a dozen impressive sources ..... took sixteen years to reach its third impression![36]

Conrad's painfully slow, though eventually spectacular, rise to popularity may be inferred from Fisher Unwin's list of impressions of *Almayer's Folly* up to 1925: first edition, 1895; second impression, 1907; third impression, 1914; fourth, 1915; fifth, 1917; sixth and seventh, 1918; eighth, 1920; ninth, 1923; tenth, 1924; eleventh and twelfth, 1925. The acceleration between 1914 and 1918 is particularly significant. In the long run, Fisher Unwin's purchase of the copyright for a mere £20 was to prove a hugely profitable investment.

Conrad proceeded with *An Outcast of the Islands*, continuing (in reversed chronological order) the Lingard Saga, the story of the establishment, decline and fall of Tom Lingard's trading empire – an ironic epic which cast sombre reflections on imperialism as a whole. Shakespeare, near the outset of his literary career, had produced a trilogy: the three parts of *Henry VI*; but the playwright had followed the customary chronological order of events. Conrad, by a process of imagination that was utterly characteristic of his nature, had begun with the end of the Lingard saga in *Almayer's Folly* and was now, with *An Outcast*, working backwards into the events prior to those described in his first novel. This habit of imagination (beginning with later events and subsequently supplying the prior parts of a sequence) was to characterise much of his subsequent work, and not just narrative strategies as a whole but also the treatment of local incidents. Delayed decoding, that procedure whereby the reader is initially confronted with an *effect* and only later infers or learns the *cause*, was a technical bridge between the ancient epical procedure (opening the narrative *in media res*) and the dislocated narratives of modernism. Frequently, in Conrad's use, it implied a powerful scepticism about orthodox conceptions of rational order in the world. It harmonised, too, with that temperamental inclination to obliquity which had led Conrad to approach the career of a British novelist via years in France and decades of voyages across far oceans.

Like *Almayer's Folly*, *An Outcast* became too long for inclusion in Fisher Unwin's Pseudonym Library. Conrad's novels frequently grew much longer than the author had initially estimated; and the predominant reason for this tendency was his imaginative integ-

rity and originality. He long manifested an imaginative resistance
to conventional plotting, being concerned with the thematics and
wider implications of the narrative. As his works used but subverted the features of romantic fiction, so also they used and subverted
standard conventions of plotting. Later, Conrad might sometimes
be seduced into prolixity (notably when writing *The Mirror of the
Sea* and *Chance*) by the method of payment for serialisation, which
was usually a matter of the word-total – so many pounds for each
one-thousand-word unit; but, at the very outset of his career, he
was not thinking in terms of serialisation.

An Outcast of the Islands was published in London on 4 March
1896. In the same month Conrad told a friend:

> The literary profession is . . . . . my sole means of support. You
> will understand, my dear Karol, that if I have ventured into this
> field it is with the determination to achieve a reputation – in
> that sense I do not doubt my success. I know what I can do. It
> is therefore only a question of earning money – 'Qui est une
> chose tout à fait à part du mérite littéraire'. ['Which is a matter
> quite apart from literary merit.'] That I do not feel too certain
> about – but as I need very little I am prepared to wait for it.[37]

His confidence in achieving 'a reputation' was confirmed by the
reviews of *An Outcast*, which predominantly were highly favourable. Some reviewers complained of the sordid and depressing
nature of the material; several found the book 'wordy', 'over-
wrought', slow and prolix; but a recurrent term was 'power'. The
Glasgow Herald, for instance, concluded:

> *An Outcast of the Islands* is a book of singular and indefinable
> power; to be read carefully, some times even with labour, but
> always beautiful in its style, rich alike in passion and in pathos.[38]

Other commentators likened the book to work by Melville, Victor
Hugo, Stevenson and Kipling; 'It is as masculine as Kipling, but
without that parade of masculinity which Kipling loves', remarked
the *Manchester Guardian*.[39] One of the longest and liveliest of the
notices was an anonymous analysis in the *Saturday Review*. Its
writer illustrated at length his thesis that Conrad repeatedly mars
vivid effects by building 'a dust-heap of irrelevant words', but
then declared:

Subject to the qualifications thus disposed of, *An Outcast of the Islands* is, perhaps, the finest piece of fiction that was published this year, as *Almayer's Folly* was one of the finest that was published in 1895.

. . . . .Only greatness could make books of which the detailed workmanship was so copiously bad, so well worth reading, so convincing, and so stimulating.[40]

Conrad sent this reviewer, who was in fact H. G. Wells, a letter of thanks and self-defence; and this marked the beginning of an uneasy and guarded friendship between the two men. Later, in *Boon* and *Experiment in Autobiography*, Wells sniped at Conrad's noble literary *persona* and his 'florid mental gestures': 'Conrad "writes". It shows.'[41] Nevertheless, in the 1890s Conrad was a genuine admirer of Wells's novels, and *The Time Machine* and *The Island of Doctor Moreau* have left their mark on various Conradian texts, notably 'Heart of Darkness' and *The Inheritors*. Furthermore, as Najder remarks, 'Although in his letters to Garnett and Unwin Conrad denied the truth of Wells's accusations [of prolixity], he must have taken them to heart, judging by the relatively economic style of *The Nigger of the 'Narcissus'*, probably begun in June [1896].'[42]

The foundations of Conrad's reputation were now firmly laid; but the financial basis of his literary career was still weak. He had received £20 for *Almayer's Folly*; for *An Outcast*, with its first British edition of 3000 copies, he received £50 plus around 11% of the proceeds.[43] The improvement in terms was not so great as to give him confidence that the maritime career could be relinquished, and until 1898 Conrad made sporadic and unavailing attempts to return to sea as a master. His inheritance from Bobrowski would not last long, in view of his gentlemanly life-style and inclination for journeys to the continent; and meanwhile his responsibilities had grown. In March 1896 he married Jessie George, a buxom young typist who was to be the mother of Borys Conrad, born in 1898, and John, born in 1906. Jessie, though unsophisticated and uncultured, proved to be a diligent, resourceful and patient wife; but, in her eventual memoirs, written after Conrad's death, she was to vent some long-suppressed resentments in anecdotes about her husband's eccentricities and irascible sensitivity. There was ill-health on both sides: Conrad was subject to gout and malarial ailments, a legacy of his African journey in 1890, in addition to severe bouts of psychological and philosophical depression; while Jessie was to be partially crippled after a bad fall in the street in early 1903.

The literary career underwent the first of many crises soon after the completion of *An Outcast*: Conrad made a series of false starts. He began a novel entitled *The Sisters*, the story of a sensitive young Slav, an artist who comes to Paris; but only the rather vapid opening was completed. Long afterwards, in *The Arrow of Gold* (published in 1919), Conrad returned to some of its themes and situations. In 1896 he also began *The Rescuer*, the final part of the Lingard trilogy, in which a relatively youthful Lingard becomes disastrously infatuated with a married woman from high society. After protracted struggles, this novel was abandoned for nearly twenty years; eventually, with the title *The Rescue*, it emerged as a serial in *Land and Water* magazine in 1919 and as a book in 1920. Thomas Moser[44] has persuasively argued that one reason for the difficulties with *The Sisters* and *The Rescuer* was that their subject, romantic love, was largely uncongenial to Conrad's temperament: isolation, incommunication, beleaguered solidarity, political intrigue and maritime crises could elicit his deeper intelligence as grand sexual passion could not.

The third false start was 'The Return', which Conrad himself recognised as 'a left-handed production':[45] it deals tortuously with the psychological trauma of a wealthy husband on learning of his wife's infidelity. In 1896-7 Conrad published in magazines the highly uneven quartet of tales ('Karain', 'The Lagoon', 'The Idiots' and 'An Outpost of Progress') which, with 'The Return', comprise *Tales of Unrest*, published by Fisher Unwin on 4 April 1898. Amid the now-customary praise from the reviewers were repeated complaints of gloom and base realism. By 1897 the magazine *Literature* would depict thus the abode of Conrad's muse:

> On the one side a door admitting us to a chamber with small, sunless windows opening on to a gloomy, monotonous landscape. On the walls prints depicting the failures and the tragedies of the world, haggard debauchees and their drunken wives, murders, suicides, and the living horrors of grinding, loveless poverty. Bookshelves filled with vast tomes of psychology leading nowhere and teaching nothing. . . . . [46]

In such commentaries there was a tendency for Conrad to be

stereotyped as a 'naturalist' and to incur the kind of obloquy that had beset Ibsen, Strindberg and Zola: a stereotype which may well have cost Conrad many readers.

For *Tales of Unrest*, Fisher Unwin had declined to offer Conrad more than an advance of £50 on a royalty of 10% for the first 2000 copies, rising to 12½% after 2000 and 15% after 4000: the same as for *An Outcast*. Conrad had sought an advance of £100, and, disappointed by Fisher Unwin, thereafter turned to other publishers. Garnett later remarked: 'I do not blame Mr. Unwin: I am told that the sales of Conrad's three early books showed a loss, in the publisher's ledger, for many years.'[47] However, under the contract with Unwin, Conrad was entitled to 90% of magazine earnings for the tales in the volume; and he soon appreciated the improvement that this could make to his income. *Cornhill Magazine* had offered Conrad one guinea (slightly more than a pound) per 500 words for a tale, and published the 6000-word 'The Lagoon' (which contained 'lots of secondhand Conradese');[48] while, with Unwin as busy intermediary, 'An Outpost of Progress' was accepted for £45 by the new multilingual periodical *Cosmopolis* – not surprisingly, perhaps, since Fisher Unwin was the London publisher of this 'International Monthly Review'.[49] Unwin nevertheless failed to persuade *Cosmopolis* to take 'The Idiots', a dour, Maupassantesque tale of congenital subnormality, murder and suicide, but managed to place it with the aesthetically-orientated *Savoy*, whose editor, Leonard Smithers, specialised in *outré*, 'decadent' and pornographic work. Conrad, who had evidently been studying the market, said to Unwin:

> I understand they pay tolerably well (2 g[uinea]s per page?). . . . .
> If you think I am greedy then consider I am greedy for very
> little after all. And if you knew the wear and tear of my writing
> you would understand my desire for some return. I writhe in
> doubt over every line. – I ask myself – is it right? – is it true? –
> do I feel it so? – do I express all my feeling? . . . . . After all it is
> my work. The only lasting thing in the world. People die –
> affections die – all passes – but a man's work remains with him
> to the last.[50]

Predictably, no magazine would accept 'The Return', that vapid and (at 20 000 words) prolix account of adultery in high society. In Edinburgh, however, *Blackwood's Magazine* agreed to pay £40 for 'Karain', a Malay tale, on condition that the proprietor be offered the first refusal of any subsequent short story by Conrad;[51] and this inaugurated a very fruitful relationship with William Blackwood.

So, by the summer of 1897, Conrad was able to command fees of £40 to £50 for tales which would fetch further sums when collected in a book; and this at a time when the average earnings of an adult male in Britain approximated £56 per year.[52] Nevertheless, as in the years of his tutelage to Bobrowski, Conrad's expenditure would repeatedly exceed his earnings. Around the end of 1896 he had borrowed £150 from Adolf Krieger; a few months later he begged £20 from Spiridion Kliszczewski;[53] and the purgatorial process (borrowing from Peter to pay Paul, during Sisyphean labours to discharge ever-increasing debts) was to continue for seventeen years.

4.2 HENLEY, THE *NEW REVIEW* AND *THE NIGGER OF THE 'NARCISSUS'*

Conrad was seeking better terms for *The Nigger of the 'Narcissus'* than Unwin would offer, and Edward Garnett introduced the author first to Reginald Smith, of Smith, Elder & Co., whose terms indicated little improvement, and next to Sydney S. Pawling, partner of William Heinemann. Pawling was encouraging, and it was agreed that (if its editor, W. E. Henley, approved) the novel should be serialised in a magazine owned by that firm, the *New Review*, and subsequently be published by Heinemann as a book. Like Unwin's link with *Cosmopolis*, the association of Heinemann and the *New Review* could prove highly advantageous to an author: Conrad expected at least £100 for serial and book rights, and the royalty-rate proved to be good: 15% on the first 2000 copies, 20% thereafter.[54] (Via Heinemann, a deal was made with the Bachellor Syndicate for possible American serialisation – which did not materialise – and with Dodd, Mead, of New York, for issue of the book in the USA.) In London, serialisation took place between August and December 1897, and the publication of the book coincided with the appearance of the last instalment.

Some of Conrad's works were written without a particular magazine in mind; but, in the case of *The Nigger of the 'Narcissus'*, there is good evidence that the prospect of serialisation in the *New Review* considerably influenced the content of the novel. As early as October 1896, Conrad had told Unwin:

> I would like to try W. Henley with my "*Nigger*" – not so much for my own sake as to have a respectable shrine for the memory of men with whom I have, through many hard years lived and worked.[55]

Although he had begun the writing beforehand, much remained to be done after the approach to the magazine's editor was made; and Conrad had taken note of Henley's response to his previous work. 'I always had a great admiration for the man', Conrad remarked to Unwin;[56] furthermore, during the negotiations with Heinemann, Conrad told Ted Sanderson: 'I want £100 for the serial and book rights and of course some percentage on the sales. Still I will take any offer (not absurdly low) they may make because I do wish to appear in the *New Review*.'[57] Henley was pleased with Chapters I and II of *The Nigger*, commenting: 'Tell Conrad that if the rest is up to the sample it shall certainly come out in the *New Review*'; and Conrad, in the eventual 'Author's Note' to the novel, quoted these words and termed them 'The most gratifying recollection of my writer's life!'[58] Conrad had remarked at the time, 'Now I have conquered Henley I ain't 'fraid of the divvle himself'; and later he conceded that *The Nigger* 'was written with an eye on him'.[59]

After that phase of abortive experiments which had included the dreary portrait of the artist as a young man (*The Sisters*) and the turgidly introspective 'The Return', and after *The Rescuer* had become stuck on a mental mudbank as tenacious as that described in its text, *The Nigger of the 'Narcissus'* was a distinctly successful new departure for Conrad. Both his previous novels, *Almayer's Folly* and *An Outcast*, had been laboured in exposition: their plots had been retarded by lengthy retrospective sequences, and the scene-setting had attained its cumulative effect largely by repetitive evocation of the oppressive gloom and futile fecundity of the jungle. With *The Nigger*, it was as though Conrad had emerged imaginatively from sombre forests into fresh sea air and sunlight. *The Nigger* can be seen as a sequence of descriptive set-pieces – there is still some sense of labour and of descriptive excess – but this time there is contrast, variety, rapid impressionistic immediacy; it is much more cinematic, the narrator's vision being diversely mobile and wide-ranging, now in the forecastle among the quarrelling men of the watch, now on the poop with the officers, sometimes recording with dry humour the discords of the crew, sometimes observing with Olympian detachment the passage of the *Narcissus* across the oceans. It is full of contrasts between noise and silence, darkness and light, storm and calm. Conrad's love of thematic density here becomes intensified in scenes which shimmer between realism, allegory and symbolism. The narrative of the voyage is partly a commemorative tribute to the great days of sail, partly a moral and political allegory of the ways in which a community may be subverted from within by egotism and duplicity, and partly a series of symbolic tableaux epitomising the price and value of the work ethic, the duties and hardships of the sea in contrast to the demeaning pressures of the land, and the right and wrong ways to respond to the threat of death. Conrad has found a way to give a sea-story not only engrossing vividness but also a wealth of moral, psychological and political implications. In *The Nigger* he has begun that great sequence of maritime tales which would include 'Typhoon', 'The Secret Sharer' and *The Shadow-Line*.

If we seek the reasons for this sudden development in his impressionistic vigour and freedom, one is that Conrad had learnt from those reviewers who had complained of the monotony and prolixity of the previous novels; in particular, he had taken to heart Wells's complaints about the rhetorical excess and tautology of *An Outcast*. Another reason is that during his voracious reading, Conrad had encountered Stephen Crane's *The Red Badge of Courage*, a brilliantly original impressionistic account of the initiation of young soldiers into the trial by ordeal of warfare. Later, Conrad conceded the thematic similarities between the two texts, with their shared interest in team psychology, the challenge of death and the testing of courage.[60] On 'literary impressionism' Conrad was equivocal, sometimes talking as though it were a superficial mode which failed to probe the inner meaning of events, and at other times praising Crane with apparently emulous and unreserved enthusiasm;[61] but on at least one occasion he declared himself an 'impressionist from instinct'.[62]

A feature of *The Nigger* which runs counter to the more radical insights of his previous novels, and which may seem wayward if we look ahead to 'Heart of Darkness' and *Nostromo*, is the vigorous

and sometimes militant Toryism. The officers of the crew are a
sterling team of British seafarers; Donkin, who foments mutiny, is
a parody-socialist; the negro Wait, as his name indicates, is a
weight or burden to the white man and the ship; trade-unionism
is implicitly scorned; even Samuel Plimsoll's reformers are
satirised; and England, though glimpsed as a place of sordid
commerce, is hailed oratorically as the 'ship mother of fleets and
nations', 'the great flagship of the race – stronger than the storms,
and anchored in the open sea'. Conrad's complex nature certainly
included some very traditional Toryism (a nostalgia for the 'organic
community' and the squirearchy of unpartitioned Poland) and
some deep respect for Britain and her mercantile marine; but in
The Nigger that Toryism takes on a polemical vigour (and, at
times, a harshness) which the earlier works had not portended.
His new novel reflects, in part, the mood of imperialistic enthusiasm which reached a peak of fervour in 1897, the festive year of
Queen Victoria's Diamond Jubilee. But, in particular, the themes
of *The Nigger* harmonise remarkably well with those of William
Ernest Henley. In the magazines which he edited, the *Scots
Observer* (later *National Observer*) and the *New Review*, as well as in
his volumes of essays and poems, Henley – the friend and
admirer of Kipling – advocated a virile imperialism and a scorn of
'sentimentality' and 'philanthropy'. One of his most famous
poems, 'Invictus', declared:

> In the fell clutch of circumstance
>   I have not winced nor cried aloud.
> Under the bludgeonings of chance
>   My head is bloody, but unbowed.
>
> Beyond this place of wrath and tears
>   Looms but the Horror of the shade,
> And yet the menace of the years
>   Finds, and shall find, me unafraid.
>
> It matters not how strait the gate,
>   How charged with punishments the scroll,
> I am the master of my fate:
>   I am the captain of my soul.[63]

It is not surprising that the author of these lines should give a
warm welcome to a text which defines the seamen's sympathy

with the duplicitous and mortally fearful Wait as a vicarious and demoralising form of self-pity; a text which pays tribute to the heroic stoicism of Singleton and the untiring vigilance of the ship's captain. Henley, ebullient and pugnacious in spite of the years of excruciating disease which had cost him one leg and scarred the other, would have smiled on the determination with which Mr Creighton, his leg smashed in the storm, continues uncomplainingly to do his duty on the *Narcissus*. (He might, however, have winced to find that the thieving villain of the voyage bears the surname of the editor's friend and collaborator, H. B. Donkin.) The *New Review* argued that the British 'ship of State' needed a captain which was not 'the shifting majority' but the monarch with her 'ripe judgment, sagacity, and decision' and her capacity to appeal to 'the national character';[64] and the political allegory of *The Nigger of the 'Narcissus'* harmonised well with such rhetoric. The novel's caustic treatment of the fomenting of mutiny ('they dreamed of the time when every lonely ship would travel over a serene sea, manned by a wealthy and well-fed crew of satisfied skippers') and of the 'demoralizing' effect of sympathy with Wait ('Through him we were becoming highly humanized, tender, complex, excessively decadent') chimed with Henley's conviction that socialism tended 'to weaken the fibre of men and destroy their individuality'[65] and with the attacks on decadence which had been made in the columns of his magazines – notably the denunciation of Oscar Wilde in the *Scots Observer* of 5 July 1890; Henley harboured 'an organic loathing' of 'all Liberalism'.[66] The lyrical tribute, near the end of *The Nigger*, to England as the 'ship mother of fleets and nations' echoes the sentiments and imagery of Henley's popular ode, *'Pro Rege Nostro'*, which invokes England as the 'Mother of ships whose might. . . . . / Is the fierce old Sea's delight'.[67]

In its themes, implications and ethical tone, *The Nigger* is closer to the spirit of Rudyard Kipling's work than is any other text of Conrad's. This Kiplingesque tone emerges strongly in Chapter 2:

> Donkin's insolence to long-suffering Mr Baker became at last intolerable to us, and we rejoiced when the mate, one dark night, tamed him for good. It was done neatly, and with great decency and decorum, and with little noise. . . . . [I]n truth, no great harm was done, even if Donkin did lose one of his front teeth.[68]

Conrad's admiration for Kipling was normally a guarded one; and if, in *The Nigger*, that guard seems to be uncharacteristically lowered, one reason may be that Kipling was a prominent member of the 'Henley Regatta': Henley had befriended Kipling and had published the *Barrack-Room Ballads* which largely established the young writer's reputation.

Conrad thus amply atoned for the time when Henley had found himself unable to read more than sixty pages of *Almayer's Folly*.[69] Partly by coincidence, partly by design, *The Nigger of the 'Narcissus'* offers, from the whole of Conrad's output, probably the clearest instance of a text ideologically modified by the immediate circumstances of magazine publication. It is well known that the circumstances of serialisation obliged Thomas Hardy to bowdlerise the more sexually-controversial passages of *Tess of the d'Urbervilles* and of *Jude the Obscure* so as not to offend the readers of the *Graphic* and *Harper's Magazine* respectively, though he restored the intended text to the book versions. Such knowledge may give the impression that periodical publication generally tended to impose the grip of conventionality on aspiring writers; but generalisations are misleading, given the diversity of available magazines and their editorial policies. Admittedly, no periodical would take Conrad's 'Falk', which deals with cannibalism among white seamen; but there was no dilution of his ferocious satire on imperialism, 'An Outpost of Progress', when it appeared in *Cosmopolis*; and, when we consider the oaths and expletives of the characters in *The Nigger of the 'Narcissus'*, it is noticeable that there were more oaths in the serial text than in the book version. Henley, whose hobby was the collection of obscene terms,[70] was far less likely to be troubled by the crew's swearing than was the reviewer in the *Daily Telegraph*, who suggested that Conrad (as a writer of the naturalist school) was inclined to call a spade not an agricultural implement but a bloody shovel.[71] William Heinemann himself had demurred, as Conrad learnt:

> Heinemann objects to the *bloody's* in the book. That Israelite is afraid of women. I didn't trust myself to say much in Pawling's room. Moreover Pawling is a good fellow. . . . . So I struck 3 or 4 *bloody's* out.[72]

Henley was also willing to publish, as a coda to the serial, the very important 'Author's Note', in which Conrad defended his aims and methods ('My aim is, before all, to make you *see*'), whereas Heinemann declined to publish it in the book version. Another factor is that even as fiercely opinionative an editor as Henley was, in editorial practice, more catholic than might be expected: the *New Review* gave hospitality in its pages not only to Conrad and Stephen Crane but also to H. G. Wells, Henry James (*What Maisie Knew*), Arthur Morrison (*A Child of the Jago*), Arthur Symons, Paul Valéry and W. B. Yeats; just as *Cosmopolis*, fostered by the Liberal supporter, Fisher Unwin, was happy to offer its pages to the anti-Liberal Kipling, whose 'Slaves of the Lamp' preceded the instalments of 'An Outpost of Progress'.[73]

Throughout his lifetime, Conrad was an assiduous (indeed, at times, obsessive) reviser of his own texts. Whenever an opportunity arose, he would tinker with paragraphs, phrases, and tiny details of punctuation. One disadvantage of serial publication was that the division into instalments sometimes breached Conrad's artistic intentions: thus, when he heard that 'An Outpost' would have to be divided between two issues of *Cosmopolis*, he observed:

> I told the unspeakable idiots that the thing halved would be as innefective [*sic*] as a dead scorpion. There will be a part without the sting – and the part with the sting – and being separated they will be both harmless and disgusting.[74]

And of *The Nigger*, Conrad remarked: 'The instalment plan ruins it'.[75] On the other hand, one advantage was that serial publication often provided Conrad (and helpers like Sanderson and Galsworthy) with an additional opportunity for proof-checking and revision, so that the book material would have had a double vetting before its appearance. The text would also be 'corrected' and tailored to 'house style' by house editors at each stage; and compositors, sometimes deliberately, but often inadvertently, would introduce their own minor variations. Of the numerous small differences between the serial text and the book text of *The Nigger* in 1897, not all are of Conrad's making; and when they are probably Conrad's, it must be said that his second thoughts are not always an improvement on his first. For instance, in the tribute to England that we have quoted previously, the serial text gives:

> A ship the mother of fleets and nations: the great flagship of the race – stronger than the storms, and anchored in the open sea.

The book, however, gives:

> A ship mother of fleets and nations! The great flagship of the
> race; stronger than the storms! and anchored in the open sea.[76]

'A ship mother' may be an improvement on 'A ship the mother',
but the exclamation-marks of the later version give an excitedly
rhetorical tone to a phrasing which in the earlier text seems more
persuasively deliberate and controlled. Again, the serial text describes Mr Baker's unfriendly sister thus: 'Quite a lady. Married to
the leading tailor of a little town, a leading Liberal, who did not
think his seaman brother-in-law quite respectable enough for
him.' In the book, 'seaman' becomes 'sailor', a trivial difference,
but 'a leading Liberal' becomes 'and its leading politician', which
weakens the anti-Liberal theme of a novel which has criticised
reformers and 'Plimsoll men'.[77] On the whole, Conrad was well
served by the *New Review* printing, and it did not display massive
discrepancies of the kind that would occur when some later
works (most notably *The Secret Agent*) suffered editorial abridge-
ment for serialisation.

When the first trade edition was issued by Heinemann in
December, Conrad anxiously studied the reviews. They were
numerous, often prominent and lengthy; and, in the main, they
were gratifying. True, the *Daily Mail* complained 'The tale is no
tale . . . . . There is no plot'; certainly the *Daily Telegraph* added 'It
is not a story at all, but an episode'; Arthur Symons obtusely
alleged that it lacked a governing idea; and Harold Frederic found
a lack of 'human interest'.[78] But the *Glasgow Herald* said: 'We have
nothing but the highest praise for this distinguished contribution
to modern literature'; the *Spectator* spoke of the 'extraordinarily
vivid picture of life' offered by this uncompromising 'writer of
genius'; and the London *Star* called it, 'Assuredly one of the most
powerful and extraordinary books of the year'.[79] Arthur Quiller-
Couch, the novelist and eminent critic, wrote personally to Conrad
to offer his praise; W. H. Chesson submitted a generous and
perceptive tribute; and Stephen Crane (whom some reviewers
saw as an influence on *The Nigger*) sent an enthusiastic letter.[80]
Pawling had introduced Conrad to Crane, and their meeting
rapidly burgeoned into a warm friendship which was to be
broken only by Crane's early death in 1900. *The Nigger of the
'Narcissus'* was, in the long term, to be regarded as one of

Conrad's major texts: the first novel in his decade of brilliance, 1897–1907. In the short term, the *Spectator's* reviewer was accurate in his claim that '[Conrad's] choice of themes, and the uncompromising nature of his methods, debar him from attaining a wide popularity'.

In retrospect, however, we can observe that Conrad repeatedly inflected his sea-tales so as to flatter a patriotic British readership. The voyage of the real *Narcissus* had terminated not in London but at Dunkirk; by changing the place of landfall to England, the novel provides a cue for the patriotic paean. Again, the real pilgrim-ship *Jeddah*, whose cowardly officers deserted the stricken vessel and its Muslim pilgrims, had a British master; but when Conrad used the same incident in *Lord Jim*, while changing the ship's name to *Patna*, the callous master was depicted as a gross and vulgar German. 'Youth' is largely based on the disastrous voyage of the *Palestine* (the *Judea* in the tale), and Marlow salutes the heroic and conscientious labour of the English crew:

> What made them do it. . . . . ? [I]t was something in them, something inborn and subtle and everlasting. I don't say positively that the crew of a vulgar French or German merchantman wouldn't have done it, but I doubt it. And it wouldn't have been done in the same way. There was a completeness in it, something solid like a principle, and masterful like an instinct – a disclosure of something secret – of that hidden something, that gift of good or evil that makes racial difference, that shapes the fate of nations.[81]

In reality, the hard-working crew of the *Palestine* consisted of a black seaman from St Kitts, a Belgian, an Irishman, two men and a boy from Devon, three men from Cornwall, and a Norwegian; while the officers were an Englishman, an Irishman and (of course) a Pole.[82] The tale, by postulating a courageous British crew, inscribes the process of patriotic myth-making. Conrad tended to idealise the traditional and professional morality of the British Merchant Navy; the courage and integrity that he celebrated were often real enough, but were not racial prerogatives of Englishmen; and he was inclined to elide the historic instances of irresponsibility, baseness and brutality.

4.3 THE BLACKWOOD PHASE: 'YOUTH', 'HEART OF DARKNESS' AND *LORD JIM*

In response to a suggestion by Edward Garnett, Unwin submitted the tale 'Karain' to William Blackwood; and this marked the beginning of a crucially important phase in Conrad's career. The firm of William Blackwood, based in Edinburgh, published books and a venerable conservative magazine: *Blackwood's Edinburgh Magazine*, popularly known as *Maga*. So Conrad was again in the position of being paid at least twice for his productions: once for serialisation, once for eventual publication in book form. Over the years, the following items appeared in the pages of *Maga*: 'Karain', 'Youth', 'Heart of Darkness', *Lord Jim*, 'The End of the Tether', and two chapters of *The Mirror of the Sea*. The firm published in 1900 the book of *Lord Jim* and in 1902 the volume *Youth: A Narrative, and Two Other Stories*. Garnett had noted that since *Blackwood's Magazine* frequently published both fictional and factual material on 'outposts of empire', travels and explorations, Conrad's work might well be deemed appropriate.

The firm was patriarchal and paternalistic, taking a close and benevolent interest in its authors. The William Blackwood who dealt with Conrad in the 1890s was the third William Blackwood and the fifth editor in succession; in his sixties, he had served the family's firm for forty years. (He was the son of John Blackwood, who had befriended Thackeray and published most of George Eliot's novels.)[83] His relationship with Conrad was to be characterised by remarkable courtesy, patience and generosity; he not only paid Conrad well, but was sympathetically flexible and trusting during a period when the author experienced extreme and entangled financial difficulties. Blackwood agreed, for instance, to stand surety to enable Conrad to borrow £250 from his bankers (the loan being linked to a life insurance policy), at the same time lending Conrad £50 which the author took years to repay.[84] Repeatedly, in this period around the turn of the century, Conrad was borrowing from one person in order to clear a debt to another. Of his earnings from Blackwood, £150 repaid Adolf Krieger, who was in urgent need of the funds he had lent to Conrad years before. The author endeavoured to explain to William Blackwood his recurrent financial troubles:

[T]here is in me yet some of the unreasonable Jack ashore spirit, and not a little of that truly Polish hopefulness which nothing either nationally or individually has ever justified. In extenuation I may only say that my ambarrasments [*sic*], worrying and humiliating, did not arise from any personal extravagance. I've taken up certain obligations which are heavier than I expected. It is a poor excuse enough. . . . .[85]

From the start, Blackwood had seen that Conrad was an author who would bring lustre to the house, even though he might not be profitable for a long time to come. His London agent, William Meldrum, whose office was in Paternoster Row, described Conrad and his work with affection and enthusiasm. After a luncheon at the Garrick Club in March 1898 he wrote to the head of the firm:

I was so glad you could meet Crane and Conrad – the two foremost of the youngest writers just now, and types of the men we want to get round the firm.[86]

Later, in January 1899:

His long story [*The Rescue*] costs two years' work. He *may* get £400 out of it, not more. And we see what he does besides his long story – two or three short stories each year, bringing in at the most £100. That means that his total income from his work doesn't exceed £300. Of course he doesn't attempt the impossible by living in London on that, but even in the country it must be difficult always to put his hand on money, if he hasn't any private capital. And I think it very splendid of him to refuse to do any pot-boiling and hope, for him and for ourselves too, that it will pay him in the long run.[87]

So, in the early stages of the relationship, from 1897 to 1900, Conrad made clear his pleasure to be writing for *Blackwood's*, his sense of joining an honoured company, and his gratitude for the friendly consideration shown him by both Blackwood and Meldrum. They, on their side, were shrewdly appreciative of Conrad's difficulties but also of the author's genius and artistic integrity; they encouraged him by their letters of congratulation on his works and by their readiness to be flexible in payments so as to advance him money at times of crisis. Both recognised the distinction of 'Youth', 'Heart of Darkness' and *Lord Jim*; and, in the case of the last of these works, displayed astonishing patience. Conrad had initially promised them that *Lord Jim* would be a short story of 20 000–25 000 words (equivalent to two instalments), a companion-piece to 'Heart of Darkness', and that these two tales would, together with 'Youth', make a single volume of thematically-linked narratives. In all three, Marlow is prominent as the reminiscing narrator; all three deal with the passage from innocence to bitter experience, with the conflict between romance and realism, with a journey into the exotic and perilous, and with absurd and tragic aspects of the imperial ambition. But *Lord Jim* grew and grew as Conrad wrote it, and serialisation in *Maga* had begun well before the end was in sight; so the instalments extended for month after month, eventually straddling the issues of the magazine from October 1899 to November 1900. The publisher nevertheless accommodated patiently this development; he arranged for *Lord Jim* to appear as a book by itself, and then waited for Conrad to furnish a tale to complete the originally-planned collection – of which 'Youth' and 'Heart of Darkness' had been already set in type. Eventually Conrad provided 'The End of the Tether', an inferior, diffuse tale, which was serialised from July to December 1902 and enabled Blackwood to publish the long-delayed *Youth* volume. Payment was generous: for *Lord Jim* Conrad received £300 for the serial, £200 advanced on royalties of approximately 17% for the book, and £30 (advanced on royalties of 15%) for the Canadian rights negotiated by the firm.[88] The attitude of Blackwood and Meldrum to Conrad is well epitomised in this letter that Meldrum sent to his employer in February 1900, as *Jim* unwound its unpredicted length:

> On my return from Edinburgh I got a letter from Conrad that he was ill, and knowing the nervous condition of the man I delayed pressure on him to wind up 'Jim'. I am sorry that the length of 'Jim' doesn't suit *Maga* which I can well understand; but, on the other hand, it makes it a more important story – it is a great story now – and in the annals of *Maga* half a century hence it will be one of the honourable things to record of her that she entertained 'Jim'.[89]

The Blackwood phase had enabled Conrad to produce some of his finest work, and later he would look back with affectionate nostalgia to his association with that company; though Blackwood himself had some grounds for feeling that Conrad had not fully kept his part of their bargain. Late in 1901 Blackwood was offered 'Falk', but not surprisingly (given that other editors, too, had flinched from its silent heroine and its frank treatment of cannibalism) declined it; 'The End of the Tether' had proved, after acceptance, disappointingly diffuse; then Conrad offered one of his worst tales, 'The Brute', which was properly rejected. Although *Maga* did publish part of *The Mirror of the Sea*, Blackwood drily observed: 'It is perhaps not Mr Conrad at his best.'[90] There were other reasons for a cooling of the relationship. As Jocelyn Baines remarks, '*Blackwood's* was a conservative, traditionalist magazine that liked to give its readers good fare in masculine story-telling';[91] and if a 'masculine' story is a 'rattling good adventure-yarn', Conrad's analytic sophistication must have taxed the patience of many readers, just as his tardiness and unreliability in producing copy must have taxed the patience of the publisher and his printers. Another factor was Conrad's curt announcement to the firm in 1903 that J. B. Pinker, literary agent, was henceforth to be his intermediary: this breached the sense of a gentlemanly and paternalistic relationship between publisher and author. Perhaps the main reason was that in May 1902 Conrad's sensitivities had been wounded by an interview during which William Blackwood, declining to become involved in yet another complicated financial scheme (this time entailing a loan of £300 and a further insurance policy on Conrad's life), had felt obliged to remind him that the firm had already been generous – without any certainty of eventual profit to an author whose yarns were inclined less to rattle than to lengthily trickle. This had provoked from Conrad a long and dignified letter of self-justification, in which he declared:

> I am conscious of having pursued with pain and labour a calm conception of a definite ideal in a perfect soberness of spirit.
>   That strong sense of sober endeavour and of calm conception has helped me to shake off the painful impression I had, notwithstanding your kindness, carried away from our interview. I don't – in the remotest degree – mean to imply that you wished to crush me. Nothing's further from my thought; but you are aware, I hope, that your words carry a considerable weight with me; and now I have no longer the buoyancy of youth to bear me up through the deep hours of depression. I

have nothing but a faith – a little against the world – in my reasoned conviction. . . . .

I am long in my development. What of that? Is not Thackeray's penny worth of mediocre fact drowned in an ocean of twaddle? And yet he lives. And Sir Walter [Scott], himself, was not the writer of concise anecdotes I fancy. And G. Elliot [*sic*] – is she as swift as the present public (incapable of fixing its attention for five consecutive minutes) requires us to be at the cost of all honesty, of all truth, and even the most elementary conception of art? But these are great names. I don't compare myself with them. I am *modern*, and would rather recall Wagner the musician and Rodin the Sculptor who both had to starve a little in their day – and Whistler the painter who made Ruskin the critic foam at the mouth with scorn and indignation. They too have arrived. They had to suffer for being 'new'. And I too hope to find my place in the rear of my betters. But still – my place. My work shall not be an utter failure because it has the solid basis of a definite intention – first: and next because it is not an endless analysis of affected sentiments but in its essence it is action (strange as this affirmation may sound at the present time) nothing but action – action observed, felt and interpreted with an absolute truth to my sensations (which are the basis of art in literature) – action of human beings that will bleed to a prick, and are moving in a visible world.

This is my creed. Time will show.[92]

Conrad hoped that this letter would eventually be quoted by 'one or two of my young faithfuls'; in course of time, many 'faithfuls', young and old, have gladly complied.

Of the breach with William Blackwood, Jocelyn Baines has remarked:

From the personal point of view it was sad but, even if material necessity had not forced the issue, an estrangement was perhaps inevitable. Conrad's talent was not suited to the pages of 'Maga' and he would soon have been in the position either of making concessions to his medium or of having his work rejected.[93]

That judgement rings true, but it generates a paradox. The truth is evident to anyone who now turns the pages of *Blackwood's*

Magazine for that period. It looks staid, sober, rational and unadventurous; and the fictional contributions are often mediocre. Representative writers are Neil Munro, author of *John Splendid: A Highland Romance*, and 'Zack' (Gwendoline Keats), author of *On Trial*: competent writers of conventional fiction; writers who would not last. Henley's *New Review*, as we have seen, offered a galaxy of innovatory and durable work, by Yeats, Valéry, James and Crane; the *Saturday Review* for the 1890s (under Frank Harris's bold editorship) featured reviews by George Bernard Shaw, Max Beerbohm and H. G. Wells, together with essays by Arthur Symons and Cunninghame Graham; while the *Savoy*, edited by Symons, provided a salon for the aesthetes. *Maga*, by contrast, was stolid and unadventurous, and Meldrum was right to argue that it needed an infusion of new, young blood. The paradox, however, is that it was in the pages of the staid, conservative *Maga* that there first appeared not only one of the most sinuously exploratory of Conrad's novels, *Lord Jim*, but also Conrad's most superb and daring achievement of all – the novella 'Heart of Darkness', so uncompromisingly radical and progressive in its techniques and in its ruthless insights into imperialism and the hubris of human endeavour. Yet its author was the man who had declared to William Blackwood (in disagreement with the proprietor's pleasure at a new type-fount for the magazine), 'I am "plus royaliste que le roi" – more conservative than Maga'.[94] The paradox dissolves, nevertheless, when we consider its larger context.

Given that he was largely concerned with the congeniality of the material for his magazine-readers, Blackwood showed sound judgement. His enthusiasm for 'Youth' is easily understandable. This was a concise, colourful and eventful tale, in reminiscential form, of a first voyage to the orient: storms, fire at sea, shipwreck, landfall; told with panache and a diversity of tones – now ironic, now drily humorous, now lyrical and romantic, now sentimental. It continued the advance towards manifold dexterity that had been marked in *The Nigger of the 'Narcissus'*; and Conrad had discovered a valuable problem-solving asset: Marlow as a character who could also act as intermediary narrator. In *The Nigger*, as some reviewers had pointed out,[95] the narratorial viewpoint was inconsistent: there the ostensible narrator had sometimes been a humble crewman, sharing the crew's superstitious doubts, uncertainties and limited knowledge of the situation, and some-

times a philosophically-minded and rhetorically-ambitious omniscience, enjoying the omniscient narrator's traditional freedom to
roam through characters and eavesdrop on inner thought-process-
es. Conrad needed a technique which would permit him consistently to enact both *limited* knowledge and *extensive* knowledge.
The invention of Marlow as protagonist and story-teller solved
the problem. The situation of limited knowledge could be represented by the younger Marlow, the inexperienced seaman on the
doomed ship; the situation of extensive knowledge could be
represented by the older, mature and experienced Marlow, portrayed as telling the tale of his younger self. Conrad could now
consistently offer a diversity of knowledge, a diversity of tones,
and a clear establishment of ironic distance between the events
recalled and the present situation of the person doing the recalling.
As Charles Marlow was patently a character and not Joseph
Conrad speaking authorially, Conrad gained a new freedom to
advocate many views without thereby exposing himself to criticism for their advocacy. Naturally, therefore, Marlow – the fullest,
most intelligent and most convincing of all Conrad's characters –
would recur as intermediary narrator in 'Heart of Darkness', *Lord
Jim* and (much later, declining into garrulity) in *Chance*; while
other tales in which Marlow was not present by name would use
a similar pattern of a tale-within-the-tale, an experienced ex-
seaman recounting the adventures of a younger self. The oblique
narrative technique of a tale-within-the-tale is an ancient literary
convention, widely used in Conrad's day (by his correspondents
James, Wells, Kipling and Cunninghame Graham, for example)
and traceable back far beyond Chaucer's *Canterbury Tales* to the
epics of Virgil and Homer, which so often incorporate sequences
of events narrated by individual characters. Conrad made the
device distinctively his own: it became peculiarly appropriate to
his need to voice both corrosive scepticism and beleaguered
affirmation, to express both the sense of isolation and the need for
solidarity, and to make conspicuously problematic the very process of narration itself. Not least, the technique whereby a
seasoned voyager reminisces to a sympathetic group of professional men was, at its simplest, congenial and appropriate to a
clubmen's and travellers' magazine like *Blackwood's*.

 In the case of 'Heart of Darkness', though, the same oblique
narrative format is used, but to much more radical and searching
effect than was the case with 'Youth'. Indeed, when one looks at

the later tale (there entitled 'The Heart of Darkness') in the pages of *Blackwood's*, the effect is, at first, like seeing a shark in a carp-pond or an octopus among minnows. It makes some of the surrounding material look slight and very vulnerable. The issue for March 1899, for instance, contains an article entitled 'An Unwritten Chapter of History: the Struggle for Borgu', which remarks:

> The men are armed with Lee-Mettords, and the little bush-fighting that was done against Lapai and elsewhere proved the superiority of the hard bullet over that used in the Sniders. The soft bullet is apt to break up when volleys are fired into bush where natives are hiding; but the Lee-Metford projectiles went through the cover so completely that the hidden party always ran before our men could get close. . . . .[96]

This article accompanies the very episode of 'Heart of Darkness' in which the 'pilgrims' empty their futile rifles into the bush, and in which the corrupted Kurtz, the former emissary of progress and civilisation, scrawls 'Exterminate all the brutes!' Conrad himself had had some fears that the tale might prove to be too radical for the tastes of *Maga*, given that before submitting he had promised Blackwood, somewhat disingenuously, 'It is a narrative after the manner of [Y]outh. . . . . The criminality of inefficiency and pure selfishness when tackling the civilizing work in Africa is a justifiable idea'.[97] What made this explanation disingenuous was, obviously, that 'Heart of Darkness' was far more sophisticated and sceptical than 'Youth', and criticised not merely 'inefficiency and pure selfishness when tackling the civilizing work' but the very basis of all such work: again and again the tale asks by what right people of one colour dare to impose themselves on people of another:

> The conquest of the earth, which mostly means the taking it away from those who have a different complexion or slightly flatter noses than ourselves, is not a pretty thing when you look into it too much.[98]

True, Marlow speculates that imperialism might be redeemed by 'An idea at the back of it': but even this tenuous speculation is mocked by the subsequent narrative's portrayal of the corruption and derangement of Kurtz, the idealist with imagination, who is so deliberately made a product of all Europe, including England: 'All Europe contributed to the making of Kurtz.'

In fact, not only was Meldrum enthusiastic about this 'wonderful' tale, as he termed it; but also William Blackwood himself was so impressed that even when ill in bed, he wrote to congratulate the author:

> It is very powerful and a wonderful piece of descriptive word painting with the weird African nightmare sensation sustained all through in a marvellous manner.[99]

Blackwood's conservatism did not blind him to the intensity of the tale; nor should it have done, since *Maga* itself was no jingoistic magazine but, in its political columns, often looked coolly and critically on the hypocrisies and follies of imperialism. In any case, 'Heart of Darkness' was such a complex, multivalent tale that many meanings – ambiguous, paradoxical and even contradictory, and not readily reducible to any one political ideology – could be elicited from it. Hence the diversity of the reviewers' responses. Garnett declared that the tale dealt with the

> deterioration of the white man's *morale*, when he is let loose from European restraint, and planted down in the tropics as an 'emissary of light' armed to the teeth, to make trade profits out of the 'subject races'[;]

but the *Manchester Guardian* said:

> [I]t must not be supposed that Mr Conrad makes attack upon colonisation, expansion, even upon Imperialism.[100]

Critical responses to the *Youth* volume (which contained 'Heart of Darkness') sounded the by-now-familiar gamut, with high praise predominating; but, after a promising start, sales for Blackwood soon declined: from 3150 copies (a six-shilling edition, first impression of November 1902) to 1050 (second impression, February 1903) and just 525 copies (third, November 1909). Again, the later sales indicate the happy ending to the story of Conrad's fortunes: the two-shilling edition of 1919 sold 15 750 copies.[101]

In 'Heart of Darkness' Conrad had developed to an extreme of thematic and symbolic complexity the basic method that he had been following from *Almayer's Folly* onwards: that of taking the ingredients of popular romantic fiction (and even of boys' adventure-tales) and submitting them to unconventionally realistic, reflective and ironic treatment. In the 1950s the same procedure enabled William Golding, an admirer of Conrad, to gain both a *succès d'estime* and immense sales with his powerful transformation of the materials of Ballantyne's *Coral Island* into *Lord of the Flies*. Conrad was fully aware of his own method, explaining it to Blackwood as the exertion of an intense transformative imagination on material which might at first glance seem merely 'the material of a boys' story'.[102]

This method, made very explicit, became virtually the subject of *Lord Jim*, that saga of a vulnerably imaginative egoist who has been corrupted partly by the reading of adventure-tales and 'light holiday literature': Jim seeks to emulate the hero of a romantic novel, seeing his subject-people as 'like people in a book'; but reality proves tragically recalcitrant. The flaw of this novel was that though, in its first half, Conrad conducted a ferociously intense campaign against clichés of narrative, characterisation and morality by offering a vast spectrum of direct and indirect judgements of Jim and his conduct, in the latter half the pressure of romance became too strong for Conrad's cogent resistance: during the campaigns on Patusan and the love-relationship of Jim and Jewel, the critical distance between cliché and ironic analysis markedly diminishes. As Conrad wearied, the seductions of the conventional became harder for him to resist; and the age-old demands of narrative closure (crisis, anagnorisis, peripeteia, dénouement) prevailed over an imagination that was often keener in exploring and complicating problems than in resolving them – a keenness which made so many of Conrad's works much longer than he had originally intended.

The magnanimity of Blackwood, who had been disconcerted by the ever-lengthening sequence of *Lord Jim*'s instalments, is shown by his advice to Conrad not to botch the ending by rushing it:

I do not think the story loses anything by the method of telling. I would not recommend any cutting down in these three chapters merely for the sake of bringing the serial issue to an earlier close. The end must now justify the length of the story, & to hurry it up for any reason but the right one be assured would be a mistake. I therefore as heretofore leave you a free hand with regard to it.[103]

Other proprietors exercised their power to prune or mutilate the fiction they published; Conrad was fortunate to find so sympathetic a patron. Not all the reviewers would have agreed with Blackwood's endorsement of 'the method of telling'. When the book appeared, the *Manchester Guardian* and the *Speaker* felt that the apparently 'digressive' material was fully justified by its moral and psychological relevance; but the *Daily Telegraph* complained of 'the constant wandering', while the *Sketch* added:

> *Lord Jim* is an impossible book – impossible in scheme, impossible in style. It is a short character-sketch, written and re-written into infinity, dissected into shreds, masticated into tastelessness.[104]

In view of such comments, Blackwood might not have been surprised by the rapid decline in book sales between 1900 (two printings, 3150 copies) and 1904 (one printing, 525 copies).[105] The book, it may be noted, differed from the serial in several substantial respects: various meditative passages were excised by Conrad; Jim (at the time of the Inquiry) became two years younger; Cornelius became Jewel's stepfather rather than her father; and Gentleman Brown was made less grotesquely melodramatic by the omission of some phrases and the modification of others – his 'blue writhing lips' become 'blue lips', and his 'skinny earthy fingers' become 'skinny fingers'. (Many of these proof-revisions were too late for inclusion in the first American and first Canadian editions; so the process of production, correction and transmission generated a diversity of *Lord Jim*s.)[106] The devious narrative technique was, wisely, left unchanged: eventually, most of Conrad's critics were to praise its searching obliquity. By his enigma-generating procedures Conrad was soliciting the subsequent attentions of enigma-solving commentators. He thus generously laid the foundations of the academic Conradian industry, which thrives on difficulties, problems and innovations to be explained, solved and rationalised. Conrad wrote for a market, but the correspondence with Blackwood shows that he also consciously wrote for an attentive posterity.

4.4 ENTER PINKER

One reason for the breach with Blackwood, as we have seen, is that in 1903 Conrad formally advised the firm that henceforth all negotiations concerning his work should be conducted with J. B. Pinker, who, three years previously, had become his literary agent. From September 1900 until the success of *Chance* in 1914, it was James Brand Pinker (1863–1922) who, more than anyone else, ensured the maintenance of Conrad's literary career. Hueffer called him 'a blinking Bramah in the shape of Destiny'.[107] Pinker's astute business-deals with publishers, and, above all, his confidence in the writer's future – a confidence which expressed itself in vast long-term loans from the agent to his client – served as a life-line which guided Conrad from a financial quagmire into the haven of affluence.

The entry of Pinker into Conrad's world was a sign of changing times in publishing. In the 1880s, increasing professionalisation could be seen in the literary world. The Society of Authors had been founded by Walter Besant in 1882 as a form of trade union for writers, designed to promote the interests of its members by gaining better terms from publishers. (Its members numbered 68 in 1884, 900 in 1892 and 2500 in 1914.)[108] A related factor was the emergence of a number of professional literary agents, to whom Besant often referred struggling authors. The rise of the literary agent had been made virtually inevitable by the proliferation of publishers, magazines and journals, and by the increasing internationalisation of the market as a consequence of international copyright agreements: the complexity of the market provided an opening for agents as middlemen. What the agent gained was a percentage – normally 10%, sometimes more and sometimes less – of his authors' earnings (Pinker charged Conrad ten). What the author gained was, first, time – as the time-consuming matter of negotiating with potential publishers could now be left to the agent, while the author concentrated on the creative work. Secondly, there were usually financial gains, since the agent, with his detailed knowledge of the market and of contractual obligations, could usually drive harder bargains than the author. Understandably, therefore, some publishers resented the literary agent's arrival on the scene: William Heinemann, who deemed the new middleman 'generally a parasite',[109] had disdainfully declined to negotiate with Pinker about Henry James's material; consequently,

Heinemann lost the opportunity to publish further books by James. As we have noted, proprietors like Heinemann, Fisher Unwin and Blackwood had themselves been acting partly as agents in placing authors' works with magazines and with foreign publishers, and in gaining for themselves, consequently, a share of the profits. Pinker and his fellows threatened to erode such perquisites. Of the price of each book, the publisher took about half and the bookseller a third; the author, if fortunate (and alive), might receive 10–15%; Pinker, A. P. Watt and (later) Curtis Brown could sometimes increase the author's percentage at the expense of the publisher.

Henry James had initially, in 1888, been referred by Walter Besant to A. P. Watt, the agent for Wilkie Collins, Bret Harte and Rider Haggard (and subsequently for Conan Doyle, Kipling and W. B. Yeats); but by 1898 James had put his work in the hands of Pinker, and the shrewd Scot proved to be 'his staunchest ally in an increasingly complex business arena'.[110] The agent loyally negotiated on James's behalf throughout the depressing period when 'The Master' (or the 'Cher Maître', as Conrad addressed him) found that a high reputation was no guarantee of large sales. Between 1896 and 1909 James's annual income, from all his novels published by Macmillan, averaged only £12.[111] James owed his eventual affluence not to his writings but to the rentals of his family's properties in Syracuse.

Garnett had recommended Watt to Conrad, who found this agent's self-publicity vulgar. In 1899 Pinker, who also acted for H. G. Wells and for Conrad's friend Stephen Crane, offered to take over Conrad's affairs. He received a remarkably candid reply:

> My method of writing is so unbusiness-like that I don't think you could have any use for such an unsatisfactory person. I generally sell a work before it is begun, get paid when it is half done and don't do the other half until the spirit moves me. I must add that I have no control whatever over the spirit – neither has the man who has paid the money.[112]

By September 1900, however, when Conrad and F. M. Hueffer faced the problem of marketing their collaborative novel *Romance*, Pinker was invited to solve it; and a year later, when he advanced Conrad £100 for the serial rights of 'Typhoon', the author was awakened to the material security that Pinker could supply.

Conrad had constantly been borrowing from Peter to pay Paul: he had been indebted to Krieger, Kliszczewski, Galsworthy, Blackwood, Cunninghame Graham and to many humbler people (notably local tradesmen). Later Hueffer and Rothenstein provided help. There were occasional windfalls (as when the *Academy* awarded him a literary prize of fifty guineas for *Tales of Unrest*), but ever since the early days of Bobrowski's guardianship Conrad had been adept at spending or losing what he received. In 1901, for instance, his income was apparently substantial: royalties from *Lord Jim*, £400 in loans, and advances from Pinker totalling £240.[113] The total appears to place Conrad in a prosperous minority.

At that time in England and Wales taken together, only 400,000 people declared an income above £400 per year; fewer than a million earned over £160. The average income per capita was about £40 per year; average earnings were barely over £90; only 2.5 percent of the gainfully employed earned over £2 per week. . . . . Servants were cheap; the maid at the Pent [Conrad's rented home] was not paid more than £20 per year.[114]

Much of Conrad's income was, however, used to pay debts and interest; he was supporting not only himself, his wife and son, but also Jessie's relatives; and he was determined to maintain a gentlemanly life-style – smart suits, frequent trips to London and farther afield, and generous hospitality to friends and visitors. At least he was spared the expense of permanent residence in the capital itself. Pent Farm, rented cheaply at £25 per year from Hueffer (who in turn rented it from the tolerant owner), nestled in the Kent countryside near Hythe. There was no bathroom: a servant had to carry buckets of hot and cold water upstairs to the bedrooms; and the lavatory, though equipped with seating for two adults and one child, was an earth-closet in the garden.

While Pinker provided long-term loans in the hope of Conrad's eventual success, the British taxpayer provided substantial gifts of cash. In 1902, at the behest of Sydney Pawling, Henry James and Edmund Gosse (its secretary), the Royal Literary Fund gave Conrad £300; in 1904 the 'Royal Bounty Special Service Fund' donated £500; and in 1908, there was a further donation, £200, from the Royal Literary Fund. (In 1903 Will Rothenstein privately collected £200 to help the author.) Furthermore, in 1910 Conrad was awarded a Civil List Pension of £100 per annum (£50 less than W. B. Yeats was to be awarded in the following year): the pension continued until 1917, when the author was at last in a position to renounce it. He had thus, yet again, been enabled to produce his masterpieces by the taxed labours of many individuals who may never have read them. In 1905 Conrad asked Pinker to pay him a regular sum (funded partly from sales of work, the rest being loaned) of £800 per year; Pinker agreed to £600. Within two years, in addition to debts to Galsworthy and 'a lot of bills unpaid in Kent', Conrad owed Pinker £1572.[115] The extent of Pinker's gamble on Conrad's prospects may be gauged from Henry Newbolt's advice that the author should make 'a composition with [the] creditors': a private bankruptcy.[116] By 1909 his debts totalled £2250, at a time when the average annual earnings of a doctor were less than £400.[117] And sometimes the relationship between Conrad and his agent resembled that between a spoilt child and a long-suffering nanny: when the author broke his pen by dropping it from a third-floor window, he immediately wrote (from France), 'My dear Pinker / Please send me *two good* fountain pens . . . . . I want something really good.'[118]

Pinker, who was outlived by his client, survived just long enough to see his own judgement vindicated and his advances handsomely repaid from his 10% share of the receipts. By 1919 Conrad would receive over £3000 for the film rights on his work and would be attracting, from the collectors John Quinn and T. J. Wise, payments for manuscripts of early tales which were far greater than the original fees for publication of those tales; and, when J. B. Pinker died in 1922, his son, Eric, inherited the agency of a very lucrative literary estate. The debt which admirers of Conrad owe to James Brand Pinker could be summed up as follows. First, Pinker provided a financial life-line during some particularly desperate years of Conrad's career. Secondly, his nagging insistence that Conrad should regularly produce copy for the market may have exasperated his client, but it also served as a necessary goad. (Conrad once told Perceval Gibbon, 'I am going to slave like anything. . . . . And then I shall come to see you whooping and singing savage war-songs with an eagle's feather in my hair and Pinker's scalp at my waist. Amen.')[119] Next, Pinker's astuteness resulted in some unlikely coups: chief among them the placing of *The Secret Agent*, that particularly sardonic and ruthless novel, in the American magazine *Ridgway's: A Militant Weekly for God and Country*. Conrad needed publicity but was temperamentally averse to courting it; Pinker's rôle alleviated this difficulty. (Conrad was mortified when hoardings advertising the serialisation of *Nostromo* proclaimed his name 'in letters three feet long', but he had urged Pinker to ensure 'a certain amount of fuss' about the serialisation of 'Typhoon' – 'The public's so used to the guidance of Advertis[e]ment!')[120] Finally, by his requests that Conrad should prepare shortened versions of his novels to increase the chance of serial publication, Pinker was partly responsible for the textual diversity of the author's works.

Conrad's unreliability, prodigality and sensitivity led, inevitably, to some fierce quarrels with his agent; but in 1916 the author told John Quinn:

> These books [of mine] owe their existence to Mr Pinker as much as to me. For fifteen years of my writing life he has seen me through periods of unproductiveness, through illnesses, through all sorts of troubles. . . . . Pinker was the only man who backed his opinion with his money, and that in no grudging manner, to say the least of it. . . . .[121]

And, on Pinker's death, Conrad wrote to F. N. Doubleday:

> I need not tell you how profoundly I feel the loss of J. B. Pinker, my friend of twenty years' standing, whose devotion to my interests and whose affection borne towards myself and all belonging to me were the greatest moral and material support through nearly all my writing life.[122]

Pinker bequeathed an estate worth £40 000: roughly twice the value of Conrad's. Pinker's rival, A. P. Watt, bequeathed £60 000. In the same period, William Heinemann left £33 000, while another of Conrad's publishers, J. M. Dent, left £14 000. Pinker's client Arnold Bennett, who was famed for financial acumen and success, would leave £36 000 in 1931.[123] These figures help to explain the fact that the list of literary agents now fills numerous pages in the *Writers' and Artists' Yearbook*.

4.5 COLLABORATION WITH F. M. HUEFFER: *THE INHERITORS* AND *ROMANCE*

Conrad's judgements of his own writings were variable and apparently inconsistent: he was capable of denigrating a major work and extolling a minor work. Often the context explains the seeming inconsistency: when writing to friends, he could be disarmingly and excessively modest about a recent novel; when writing to publishers or to his agent, he would naturally be inclined to 'talk up' its merit and commercial value. In the main, at least until the late years of his decline, he was well able to distinguish between his truly important works and the minor material. Towards 1900, as debts mounted and royalties proved consistently disappointing, he responded to the pressures of the market-place by consciously imposing a bifurcation on his literary energies. Part of his time would continue to be given to work of integrity: to taxing, original texts which might appeal to discerning critics and, eventually, to posterity. But another part of his time would be devoted to the rapid production of material for sale: slight tales, potboilers, and, above all, the collaboration-work with Ford Madox Hueffer – 'our partnership – in crime'.[124]

What Conrad brought to the collaboration included his own prestige, based on a high proportion of favourable reviews for his earlier works, and a network of influential contacts in the literary world – Garnett, James, Wells, Cunninghame Graham, Gosse and Saintsbury among them. What Hueffer brought was his youthful energy, a mind full of fancies and speculative schemes, and a rapid facility and fluency as a writer. The collaboration had its overt and its covert aspects. Conrad and Hueffer proclaimed themselves the joint authors of *The Inheritors: An Extravagant Story* (1901) and *Romance: A Novel* (1903). A long tale, 'The Nature of a Crime', was initially published (in Hueffer's *English Review*, 1909) in the name of Baron Ignatz von Aschendrof [*sic*], though in 1924 it was to be openly accredited to the true authors. In all three cases the proclamation of joint authorship was deceptive, since there is no doubt that the bulk of the writing was Hueffer's. The covert part of their arrangement was this: although the autobiographical *The Mirror of the Sea* was advertised as only Conrad's work, six of its fifteen divisions were partly the work of Hueffer, who acted as prompter, amanuensis and elaborator; indeed, in its literary techniques, the whole book has been termed 'more Fordian than Conradian'.[125] In addition, the two writers agreed that Hueffer should stand by as 'secret sharer' to help Conrad with this and other works in emergencies, when, say, the older man was in danger of missing the deadline of a serial instalment.[126] In later life Hueffer, who was prolific in egoistic fantasies, exaggerated the extent of his contribution to Conrad's *oeuvre*. Some of his claims, nevertheless, have substantiation. He said he had contributed (without acknowledgement) to *Nostromo*, in order 'to keep the presses going' when Conrad was unwell; and part of the manuscript (about sixteen pages for Chapter 5 of Part II) is in his hand-writing. Given that in these pages the plot 'marks time', commentators are now inclined to accept Hueffer's claim that here he was no mere amanuensis but actually a creative contributor to Conrad's most ambitious novel.[127] He may also have furnished some parts of 'The End of the Tether' after much of Conrad's manuscript was destroyed when a table-lamp exploded. Hueffer certainly provided the bases of the tales 'Amy Foster' and 'To-morrow', and helped Conrad convert the latter into a one-act play.[128] Incidentally, though short of funds himself, Hueffer joined the long roll of honour of Conradian creditors.

Literary collaborations, avowed and unavowed, have a venerable ancestry: *Two Noble Kinsmen* and *Henry VIII* have both been ascribed to the joint authorship of William Shakespeare and John Fletcher. In Conrad's day, Robert Louis Stevenson joined forces with W. E. Henley to write three plays; Israel Zangwill and Louis Cowen produced *The Premier and the Painter*, a satiric novel which may well have influenced *The Secret Agent*;[129] Walter Besant and James Rice created in partnership numerous tales, novels and a play; and *The Naulahka*, a novel, bore the names of Rudyard Kipling and Wolcott Balestier. The same list, however, suggests that literary collaborations usually represent a victory of expediency over artistic integrity. Hueffer's best work is to be found not in *The Inheritors* or *Romance* but in *The Good Soldier* (1915), a sensitively analytic narrative of marital treachery: a novel in which, according to Graham Greene, 'Ford's apprenticeship with Conrad had borne its fruit, but he improved on the Master'.[130]

Hueffer, born in 1873, held promising cultural credentials. His father, Franz Hüffer (or Hueffer) had emigrated from Germany to England and had become music critic for *The Times* and the *Fortnightly Review*; his mother was the daughter of the famous Pre-Raphaelite painter, Ford Madox Brown, and the sister-in-law

of William Michael Rossetti. By the time of his meeting with
Conrad, F. M. Hueffer had published a biography of his maternal
grandfather, a mediocre novel (*The Shifting of the Fire*), collections
of fairy-tales and a book of poetry, and had embarked on the
historical novel, *Seraphina*, which was eventually to emerge with
the more 'marketable' title, *Romance*. In 1908 he became founder-
editor of the *English Review*, which, in addition to publishing items
by Conrad, helped to establish literary Modernism by giving
space to a younger generation: Ezra Pound, T. S. Eliot and D. H.
Lawrence. After serving on the battlefields of the First World War,
he changed his name in 1919 to Ford Madox Ford. As founder-
editor of *Transatlantic Review* he maintained his reputation as a
patron of important new writers, publishing work by Gertrude
Stein, E. E. Cummings, Ernest Hemingway and James Joyce.
Meanwhile, he continued, until his death in 1939, to write novels,
poems and reminiscences; his recollections of Conrad, in *Joseph
Conrad: A Personal Remembrance* (1924) and *Return to Yesterday*
(1931) were to prove unreliable but lively, as he avowedly aimed
for accuracy of *impression* rather than accuracy of *fact*.

It was Conrad who approached Hueffer with a view to collaboration.[131] He appreciated the younger man's energy and facility,
and he also needed to overcome a sense of cultural isolation.
(Jessie Conrad, redoubtable in domestic management and indus-
trious as a typist of her husband's copy, had little literary knowledge.) The first of the Conrad–Hueffer novels to be published, *The
Inheritors*, held some promise in its ideas but betrayed the promise
in the execution. A Wellsian science-fiction notion (ruthless
'Fourth Dimensionists' infiltrating the British establishment) is
combined with a topical political *roman à clef* about expediency
triumphing over decency in high places; there are traces of the
anti-colonial themes of 'Heart of Darkness' and the impending
Nostromo. The insipid character who serves as first-person narrator
tends to impart his insipidity to all he observes, and the text lacks
vigour and conviction. The book's reviewers, on the whole, were
notably lenient: although the *Daily Chronicle* felt 'bamboozled' and
the *Scotsman* complained of 'curious obscurity', the *Manchester
Guardian* found 'extraordinary delicacy', the *Daily Telegraph* com-
mended it to 'the thoughtful', and the *Daily News* deemed it a
'very interesting study'.[132] Conrad and Hueffer had reason to feel
pleased; Hueffer had gained the lustre of association with Conrad,
while the older writer had gained payment for a novel on which

Hueffer had done almost all the work. 'And poor *H* was dead in earnest!', Conrad told Garnett. 'Oh Lord. How he worked! There is not a chapter I haven't made him write twice – most of them three times over.'[133] Their method had been this: first, both men wrangled about the ideas; then Hueffer wrote; next, Conrad considered the result and they wrangled again; then Hueffer re-wrote, with Conrad adding various passages. Hueffer estimated that the book contained 75 000 words, of which 'there cannot be more than a thousand – certainly there cannot be two – of Conrad's writing'.[134] *The Inheritors* was published by Heinemann (where Garnett was now working as a reader), so Conrad had partly atoned to that firm for his failure to deliver *The Rescue*; and the collaborators shared equally the publisher's advance on royalt ies of £100, with American payments to come.[135]

In the case of *Romance*, the collaboration was less lopsided – a *'welded* collaboration', as Conrad called it;[136] though, even here, the basis of the project was a full draft of the novel by Hueffer. He showed the draft to Conrad, and the two men then began a complex process of discussion, revision and further revision; Pinker's advice on market requirements was studied, and, at the proof stage, suggestions by Galsworthy and even by Jessie Conrad were noted and used. ('I've put remarkable guts into that story', declared Conrad, explaining that Part III 'is practically my work'.)[137] This was a historical romance, set in the West Indies in the early nineteenth century, featuring pirates, a young English hero and a beautiful Spanish inamorata; and the aim was frankly commercial (an assault on the market captured by Stevenson with his adventure-novels), though both writers salved their artistic consciences by avowedly tackling the material in a craftsmanlike way. '[H]ere at least we hold something with a promise of popular success', said Conrad[138] – who had recently been in debt even to his grocer. To increase the likelihood of serialisation, both writers also produced a drastically shortened version of the novel (half the original length) for Pinker to offer to magazines – though, in the event, it was never used. The spirit of the venture is perhaps most clearly represented in a letter from Conrad to Hueffer, in which the older man notes that a Polish correspondent has asked him for an explanation of *Romance* on finding it anomalous in Conrad's *oeuvre*.

One would not be far wrong if one wrote – *"Ne voyez vous pas*

que c'est une bonne farce!!!" ["*Can't you see it's a big joke?*"] But
that would not do perhaps. Also one could write: "Le besoin de
manger, de fumer, de boire, de porter une culotte comme tout
le monde." ["The need to eat, smoke, drink, have clothes on
one's back like everyone else."] But he is not the sort of person
to believe in the Obviousness of the Incredible. I suppose the
aest[h]etic racket is the practicable answer. . . . .[139]

Once again, the reviews were on the whole generously laudatory, sometimes very enthusiastic: 'Good selling notices', said
Conrad,[140] who hoped for big sales; but, as before, a frankly
commercial venture failed to gain really lucrative rewards. In the
long run, this designedly 'popular' work was to prove far less
popular than much more taxing and complex novels like *Lord Jim*
and *Nostromo*.

Possibly Hueffer's most important contribution to Conrad's
works was actually his presence as a willing ghost-writer, should
need arise. When Conrad embarked on *Nostromo*, and when that
work steadily grew from a short tale into a vast historic panorama,
he repeatedly assured Pinker that, should death or illness prevent
the author from meeting his obligations, Hueffer was standing by
to supply material and even, if necessary, complete the novel.
This was partly Conrad's way of reassuring Pinker that the agent
would be able to recoup money advanced to the author. But there
was reassurance for Conrad, too, in this arrangement. Knowing
that Hueffer was able to step in should there be an emergency
(perhaps a serial deadline to meet), Conrad seems to have been
able to work with greater confidence and intensity. He had been
much preoccupied with life insurance policies as a security for
loans; now he was using Hueffer's good will and known powers
of literary mimicry as an *artistic* insurance policy. Hueffer's direct
contribution to *Nostromo* may only have been a few pages; his
indirect contribution, as a sustainer of Conrad during the writing
of his most ambitious novel, was inestimably greater.

4.6 THE MIRROR OF THE SEA, NOSTROMO AND T. P.'S WEEKLY

The confidence to embark on the greatest of his novels, *Nostromo*,
was provided partly by the Royal Literary Fund grant of £300,

which gave Conrad a brief financial respite, and partly by Hueffer's readiness to act as covert author should Conrad himself be prevented by death, illness or mishap from completing the work or keeping abreast of serial requirements. During this period (1902–4) the bifurcation in Conrad's creativity, in response to the rival claims of his imaginative conscience and the needs of the market, became extreme. For part of the day he might be writing, or dictating, *Nostromo*; for the rest of the day he would be dictating the reminiscences which became *The Mirror of the Sea*. Of the later work, Conrad remarked:

> I've started a series of sea sketches and have sent out P[inker] on the hunt to place them. This must *save* me. I've discovered that I can dictate that sort of bosh without effort at the rate of 3000 words in four hours. Fact! The only thing now is to sell it to a paper and then make a book of the rubbish. Hang!
> So in the day *Nostromo* and from 11 pm to 1 am dictation.[141]

Those who helped by taking the dictation included Jessie, who by now was an experienced typist of Conrad's material; Hueffer, who by his prompting and cajolery helped to elicit Conrad's recollections; and Miss Lillian Hallowes, who, to an increasing extent over the years, became Conrad's secretary. Miss Hallowes was to be paid one pound and five shillings per week, at a time when a single essay for *The Mirror of the Sea* might earn £30 from a magazine, and when Conrad expected to earn £7 per thousand words for the American serialisation of *Nostromo* – in addition to an advance for the book of £100 on royalties of 15%.[142] Another reason for the relative ease of production of *The Mirror* is that Hueffer sometimes contributed to the writing as a 'secret sharer' of the enterprise. Conrad arranged to pay him proportionately from the income.[143]

The Mirror of the Sea is variable in quality, some parts being sharp vignettes of maritime acquaintances and locations, others being pretentious passages of rhetoric about the winds of the oceans:

> The West Wind is the greatest King. The East rules between the Tropics. They have shared each ocean between them. Each has his genius of supreme rule. The King of the West never intrudes upon the recognised dominion of his kingly brother. He is a

barbarian, of a northern type. Violent without craftiness, and
furious without malice, one may imagine him seated masterfully
with a double-edged sword on his knees upon the painted and
gilt clouds of the sunset. . . . .[144]

Such inflated writing nevertheless suited the tastes of many
periodicals, for Pinker had little difficulty in placing the episodes
of *The Mirror* with a diversity of magazines, ranging from *Harper's*
and *Pall Mall* to *World Today*; even the popular penny newspaper,
Alfred Harmsworth's *Daily Mail*, printed three instalments. Indeed, there are good grounds for deeming the book of *The Mirror*
an anthology of periodical items which were designed to appeal
to editors in need of short, literary (but not too taxing),
reminiscential items related to the causes of seamanship, trade
and empire. Nostalgic romanticism came readily (sometimes too
readily) to the exiled Pole; and the mood of nostalgia was certainly
fashionable in poetry, essays and fiction during the period 1890 to
1910, largely as a reaction to rapid social changes consequent on
urbanisation and industrialisation. So *The Mirror of the Sea* was, in
the main, treated leniently by reviewers, even though, as Baines
subsequently observed,

> It lacks unity of approach or design – for instance 'The Heroic
> Age', an essay on Nelson, seems only to have been tagged on at
> the end because it happened to have been written for the
> centenary of Trafalgar – and the book is certainly far from being
> the 'very intimate revelation' which Conrad claimed. Some of
> the pieces are no more than impersonal and general essays, a
> form of writing in which Conrad was weakest. . . . . The writing,
> which has been admired, is often muddled, overstrained, and
> excessively metaphorical . . . . . 'Rulers of East and West' is
> burdened   with   the   most   elaborate   and   inconsistent
> anthropomorphism . . . . .[145]

If *The Mirror of the Sea* was one of the most magazine-orientated
productions of Conrad, *Nostromo*, though written concurrently,
was one of the *least* magazine-orientated. The contrast is stark.
This, the most ambitious, panoramic and structurally complex of
Conrad's full-length novels, is still, today, a dauntingly rich text
for readers of the book. The time-shifts, the frequent changes in
narratorial viewpoint, the highly ironic linkages of part to part

and of incident to incident, the subtle echoes of leitmotivs – all
these features ensure that *Nostromo* is far more likely to be
appreciated at a second reading of the book than at the first. Yet
this novel, with all its salient difficulties, appeared as a serial in
the popular magazine, *T. P.'s Weekly*, between 29 January and 7
October 1904. It was then a common practice (far more common
than it is today) for readers to save copies of magazines; those
who did not might well have been perplexed by the serpentine
narrative as it coiled and uncoiled during the months. Numerous
subscribers complained about the serial's difficulty; the editor did
not publish their complaints, but Conrad heard of them, and long
afterwards recalled that the magazine had serialised the novel

> to the special annoyance of its readers who wrote many letters
> complaining of so much space being taken by utterly unreadable
> stuff.[146]

The magazine's editor may not initially have realised the extent of
his gamble; like *Lord Jim*, *Nostromo* became far longer than Conrad
had originally envisaged. (*The Rescue* had failed to materialise
even though the author had been paid for its serialisation.)

That editor, T. P. O'Connor, was the Liberal Member of Parliament for Liverpool (Scotland division) and a prolific journalist;
the other magazines which he directed, the *Star* and the *Sun*,
were committed to radical Liberalism and Irish Home Rule; his
Weekly, on the other hand, was addressed mainly to the Leonard
Basts of the community – the young men on the fringes of the
middle class who wished to better themselves in their careers and
particularly in the world of literary culture. Typical articles gave
advice on how to file newspaper clippings and how to acquire
critical judgement by sampling 'touchstones' of great literature;
and the magazine offered extracts from the classics, book reviews,
literary gossip ('T.P. in His Anecdotage'), travel notes ('T.P.'s
Travel Talk') and correspondence ('T.P.'s Letter-Box'). Ironically,
the final instalment of *Nostromo*, in which Mrs Gould is told that
her husband's mine 'shall weigh as heavily upon the people as
the barbarism, cruelty and misrule of a few years back', was
accompanied by an article entitled 'How to Become a Mining
Engineer'. Unlike the more staid and ponderous literary periodicals, *T.P.'s Weekly* provided a varied, easy-to-read sequence of
short items interspersed with advertisements. Some advertisers

offered correspondence courses on 'Hypnotism, Magnetic Heal-
ing, Clairvoyance, Personal Magnetism'; the makers of 'Scrubb's
Preparation' promised that it would cleanse the hair, remove
stains from clothing, restore colour to carpets, soften hard water,
polish plate and jewellery, and ensure a refreshing Turkish bath;
and the inventor of 'Patent Nose Machines' undertook to 'improve
ugly noses of all kinds'. In such hucksters' company appeared
Conrad's massive onslaught on material interests and economic
imperialism.

O'Connor himself had been eager to capture Conrad ever since
the time in 1895 when he had read 'with rapture' *Almayer's Folly*
and proclaimed the author's genius in the 'Book of the Month'
columns of the *Weekly Sun*.[147] A fortnight before the serialisation
of *Nostromo* began, *T.P.'s Weekly* offered a tribute to Conrad's
'Youth' from its regular columnist, 'John o'London'; and on 5
February, a letter from 'M.K.S. (Enfield)' declared that 'since
Stevenson no writer has been able, save Conrad, to thrill one's
innermost emotions in a few words' – and that even Kipling
could not have written 'Youth'.[148] Conrad, however, seems to
have regarded publication in *T.P.'s Weekly* as a demeaning if
unavoidable descent into the market-place; a descent from the
heights commanded by Henley or Blackwood. He called the
magazine 'TP's horror'.[149] Formerly, he had bewailed the cutting
into instalments of 'An Outpost of Progress' and 'Heart of Darkness', and had insisted on correcting proofs; now, he gave T.P.
carte blanche to do as he wished with *Nostromo*. (He had not
forgotten that after all the efforts to compress *Romance* for
serialisation, no magazine had taken it, and the labour had been
wasted.) Conrad told Pinker:

> I have no objection to the compression of the story for the
> purpose of serial pub[on] in T.P.'s Weekly – as long as I am not
> called upon to do the compressing myself. I am willing to trust
> in that matter M[r] O'Connor's judgment, the skill of his staff
> and, most of all, *his supervision* of the process. I would stipulate
> also that no proofs be sent to me. On those conditions I am
> ready to let M[r] O'Connor have an absolutely free hand in
> making the story acceptable to his large public.
>
> I work as I can. Not very intelligently perhaps, but I trust I
> have enough intelligence to understand his point of view, and
> frankly, looking at the conditions of publication (short instal[ts]

and so on) it seems to me wise generally and of advantage even to myself. There's nothing I desire less than to appear as a portentous bore before so many readers.[150]

In complete contrast was his attitude to the prospective book version, to be published in New York and London by the American firm of Harper & Brothers:

> Whatever happens I *must* have proofs of the book. They can't do better than send them out to me from N. York. I can't let a book of mine go into the world without a careful personal revision. Let them pull off galley slips in the US – or else here if they are going to set it up here. And I *will not* put up with the American spelling in the English edition. I would rather – and I will too – fling the whole thing into the fire. Till I am sure of that they shan't get a page more out of me. Let it be clearly understood.[151]

The logic of the contrast is plain. The serial is for the immediate but ephemeral readership, and – in the case of *Nostromo* – is not the author's prime concern; but the book is directed at a more scrutinising and long-term readership: it is aimed in a trajectory towards posterity, and therefore demands 'careful personal revision'.

When writing *Nostromo*, Conrad *may* have made a few concessions to the exigencies of serialisation: a conspicuous feature of the text is the large number of recurrent tags to facilitate character-recognition. Nostromo is repeatedly the 'incorruptible', 'indispensable' or 'magnificent' Capataz de Cargadores, Mitchell is 'Fussy Joe', Don José Avellanos is the 'Elder Statesman of Costaguana', Decoud 'the boulevardier' and Viola 'the old Garibaldino'. This, however, had been a common device in novels; and it can be found even in *Almayer's Folly* (as when Babalatchi is repeatedly termed 'the statesman of Sambir'), of which serialisation was not envisaged. When we compare the serial text of *Nostromo* with the first bound edition, we find that the basic structure, with its labyrinthine complexity, remains largely unchanged. There are, however, many changes in dialogue, descriptive detail and character analysis, and Conrad has revised various specifications of time and distance in the endeavour to reduce inconsistencies. The serial contains several passages whose elimination from the book weakens locally their chapters: for instance, the description of the wretched beggars at the church doors, or Hirsch's castigation of the 'preposterous export duties' on hides.[152] Elsewhere, of course, the book effects amplification: particularly of the final episode, to which Conrad added approximately 14 000 words. Here his additions include the Marxist photographer who, in the novel's political thesis, serves a sardonically prophetic purpose. The periodical text also lacks some of the passages which subsequently were to be regarded (and frequently quoted) as key statements. For example, when Decoud is marooned on the island, the serial version lacks these lines:

> In our activity alone do we find the sustaining illusion of an independent existence as against the whole scheme of things of which we form a helpless part. Decoud lost all belief in the reality of his action past and to come. On the fifth day an immense melancholy descended upon him palpably. He resolved not to give himself up hopelessly to these people in Sulaco, who had beset him, unreal and terrible, like jibbering and obscene spectres. He saw himself struggling feebly in their midst, and Antonia, gigantic and lovely like an allegorical statue, looking on with scornful eyes at his weakness.[153]

Again, there is no counterpart in the serial to the two long reflective paragraphs which, in the book, close Chapter XI of Part Three. Those paragraphs sum up the wisdom of Mrs Gould's melancholy experience, and include the following observations:

> It had come into her mind that for life to be large and full, it must contain the care of the past and of the future in every passing moment of the present. Our daily work must be done to the glory of the dead, and for the good of those who come after. . . . . There was something inherent in the necessities of successful action which carried with it the moral degradation of the idea. She saw the San Tomé mountain hanging over the Campo[,] over the whole land, feared, hated, wealthy, more soulless than any tyrant, more pitiless and autocratic than the worst Government, ready to crush innumerable lives in the expansion of its greatness. . . . . With a prophetic vision she saw herself surviving alone the degradation of her young ideal of life, of love, of work – all alone in the Treasure House of the

World. . . . . In the indistinct voice of an unlucky sleeper lying passive in the grip of a merciless nightmare, she stammered out aimlessly the words –
"Material interests."[154]

Even these two quoted passages will serve to show how the additional material emphasises thematic connections between different parts of the narrative and provides a sombre moral and philosophical resonance. 'In our activity alone do we find the sustaining illusion of an independent existence' – but it is only a sustaining *illusion*; and even if action appears to succeed, there is 'something inherent in the necessities of successful action which carrie[s] with it the moral degradation of the idea'. Both Decoud and Mrs Gould are presented as figures trapped in nightmare, seeing through and beyond the turmoil of strife, trade and conquest which engorges the lives of the nation. As so often in this novel, Conrad has sought here to establish ironic connections between apparently contrasting characters: part of his large-scale strategy of thematic coordination, which eventually gives *Nostromo* so much of its searching and prophetic power as a text about vast historical processes.

Finally, the intensity and fine detail of Conrad's textual revisions may be seen in a comparison of the concluding lines of the novel, from the point at which Linda Viola calls out the name of Nostromo, 'Gian' Battista!' Here's the version in *T.P.'s Weekly*[155] – with the text of the advertisement which, in the same column, immediately followed the ending:

From the deep head of the gulf, full of black vapour, and walled by immense mountains from Punta Mala round to the west of Aznexa, where the obscure gringos, dead in life and living in death, guard the legendary treasure, out upon the ocean with a bright line marking the illusory edge of the world, where a great white cloud hung brighter than a mass of silver in the moonlight, in that cry of a longing heart sending its never-ceasing vibration into a sky empty of stars, the genius of the magnificent Capataz de Cargadores dominated the place.

(THE END.)

MONEY SAVED on Linen. Buy from Ireland at Factory Prices. Collars, 4s. 11d. doz.; Nursery Diaper, 4½d. yd.; Ladies'

Handkerchiefs, 2s. 3d. doz. Samples, post free. – HUTTON'S.
Room 92. Larne. Ireland.

And here is the version which appeared in the first British edition
of the book:

> Dr. Monygham, pulling round in the police-galley, heard the
> name pass over his head. It was another of Nostromo's suc-
> cesses, the greater, the most enviable, the most sinister of all.
> In that true cry of undying passion that seemed to ring aloud
> from Punta Mala to Azuera and away to the bright line of the
> horizon, overhung by a big white cloud shining like a mass of
> solid silver, the genius of the magnificent Capataz de Cargadores
> dominated the dark Gulf containing his conquests of treasure
> and love.

THE END

What Conrad would have termed a 'magazine-ish' quality can be
found in both versions: a sense of willed crescendo, a slippage
into cliché ('that cry of a longing heart', 'that true cry of undying
passion'). Nevertheless the second version is more measured and
controlled in its syntax, and the bathos of 'dominated the place'
has been vigorously thrust aside by 'dominated the dark gulf
containing his conquests of treasure and love', which by its
alliteration and rolling rhythm completes a majestically rhetorical
peroration. And the book, of course, lacks the advertisement for
Hutton's Irish Linen. That advertisement, following immediately
after the breathless crescendo of Conrad's epic, resembles a
derisory snigger at the end of a requiem mass, or a street-vendor's
cry disrupting the moment of silence before the applause for a
symphony. Yet it marks, with laconic precision, the irony of the
conditions of production of *Nostromo* and, indeed, the irony of
Conrad's whole situation as a writer for both posterity and the
literary market-place. For readers of *T.P.'s Weekly* who wish to
weep at the plight of the bereaved Linda Viola, handkerchiefs are
available at two-and-threepence a dozen (samples post free).
Readers who endorse Conrad's vision of the corruption entailed
by 'material interests', of the ways in which capitalism imposes its
injustices even on those who seek to promote justice, and of the
process by which economic imperialism perverts the lives of

rulers and ruled alike, can nevertheless purchase their collars and nursery diapers at factory prices. Hutton's advertisement helped to keep down the price of *T.P.'s Weekly*, so that more people could be tempted to read *Nostromo*; it helped to provide the funds from which the author could be paid his fee. At the core of *Nostromo*'s pessimism is the recognition that even those individuals who seek to reform and humanise a system of repeated appropriation are themselves, whether they realise it or not, servants of the very process they wish to control; and it was a recognition made by Joseph Conrad every time the nervous ordeal of his writing, the ferocious struggle for truth in phrases, was followed by the haggling over the number of pounds and shillings per thousand words. The characterisation of Gould, enslaved by the silver-mine which ensures his wealth, obsessed by that endless endeavour to force riches from darkness, must have been based partly on the predicament of Conrad himself, hewing words from blackness as a miner hews coal – only to find that the more he produces, the more he is in debt.

Initially, few commentators appreciated fully the immensity of the achievement of *Nostromo*. Some of T. P. O'Connor's readers resented the difficulty of the serial, and professional reviewers lamented the difficulty of the book. The *Times Literary Supplement* declared *Nostromo* 'an artistic mistake', 'a shapeless work'; the *Daily Telegraph* regretted 'the inability to see the wood for the trees'; the *British Weekly*, while praising the vivid realism, deemed the plot 'confused'; and the *Manchester Guardian* encountered 'an arbitrary and baffling design'.[156] Edward Garnett, however, offered in the *Speaker* a long, discriminating and keenly intelligent vindication of Conrad's methods and purposes, while the *Illustrated London News* declared: '*Nostromo* will set the seal upon Mr. Conrad's title to rank in the forefront of living novelists.'[157] Today, the text can judge its erstwhile jurors.

4.7 *THE SECRET AGENT, RIDGWAY'S* AND THE THEATRE

Conrad wrote *The Secret Agent* between February and November 1906. Pinker secured the serialisation of it in a down-market magazine which liked to expose scandals in high places: *Ridgway's: A Militant Weekly for God and Country* (October to December 1907).

Conrad remarked to Pinker: 'Ridgway's are sending me their rag. It's awful – and it don't matter in the least. I see they are "editing" the stuff pretty severely.'[158] He then revised the material extensively, adding Chapter 10 (dealing with the unmasking of Vladimir by the Assistant Commissioner) and rewriting 11 and 12: this increased the length of the text by over 26 000 words, and ensured that he would comply with Methuen's contract, which stipulated a minimum of 75 000.[159] Methuen of London published the book in September 1907. So a relatively short typescript for serialisation had been further shortened by the magazine editor and then considerably expanded for book publication. Many of the passages omitted in *Ridgway's* concern the history and circumstances of the characters; others are philosophical or 'essayistic' reflections by characters or the narrator; and various images (harassed man as tight-rope artist, muddy London as aquarium, for instance) also vanished. Emily Dalgarno has observed:

> The essayistic passages as well as the images are remarkable for their self-containment; that is they were deleted from otherwise unrevised paragraphs which still maintain unity and function in the narrative sequence.

She comments that by placing his work and the management of his affairs in the hands of a literary agent, Conrad had entered a world in which a book was primarily a commodity for the market:

> The decision meant the surrender of some control over the published text. Unlike Dickens, who accommodated himself to serial publication by listing the numbers and titles of chapters of a book which he might take nineteen months to write, Conrad was usually unable to plan either the overall length, or the subdivisions of his work before actual writing began. Not only did uncertainty over the actual length of a work complicate Conrad's relationship with Methuen in particular, but the relationship of a 'shortened' to a full-length version of the text exerted some pressure on his style.[160]

Ridgway's, in the tones of a school-teacher, introduced the serial with the following explanation which (as many reviewers had) emphasised Conrad's kinship with Kipling and Stevenson:

Joseph Conrad, the author of "Youth," "Romance," "Typhoon," etc., is a story-teller who writes literature. Like Stevenson and Kipling, his tales last because there is more of them than the bare bones of plot; there is the knowledge of men, the feeling for life. In his new novel, "The Secret Agent," there is a deal of plot and life. It is a story of diplomatic intrigue and anarchist treachery.[161]

In the abbreviated serial text of *The Secret Agent*, 'plot' gains a denuded prominence. After the first episode, each instalment is preceded by a synopsis of the story so far; and the copious illustrations by Henry Raleigh (in a style verging on caricature) solicit the reader by isolating dramatic incidents – the revelation of the mangled remains of the bomb-victim, or the stabbing of Verloc by his wife. In *Ridgway's, The Secret Agent* becomes a different novel: less resonant and subtle; a graphic thriller for rapid reading. The *Militant Weekly for God and Country* has not censored the information that Verloc's shop sells pornographic books and photographs; and the serial winds its way between advertisements for Johnson's revolvers (five dollars each), ten-cent cigars, washing machines and the unexpurgated works of Balzac.

Conrad said that the subject of *The Secret Agent* came to him when he and a friend were discussing the Greenwich Bomb Outrage of 1894 (when an actual anarchist, Martial Bourdin, had blown himself up near the Observatory), and the friend remarked, 'Oh, that fellow was half an idiot. His sister committed suicide afterwards.'[162] This 'omniscient' friend was almost certainly Hueffer, whose cousins (the Rossettis) had produced an anarchist newspaper and welcomed foreign anarchists. The memoirs of Sir Robert Anderson, former Assistant Commissioner of the police, provided further ideas. And in due course Conrad had become absorbed in the writing of a novel which showed that even in his late forties, his interest in narratological experimentation and stylistic virtuosity was still vigorous.

Although it marked a distinctive departure for Conrad, we can see that this book effects a characteristic Conradian compromise between the claims of the literary market-place and the integrity of the author as innovator. The work combines several popular genres: detective fiction; crime fiction; spy fiction; the political thriller involving anarchists or terrorists. The originality of the treatment lay in the Conradian narrative obliquity (particularly in the time-shifts and the use of delayed decoding) and in the sustained ironic tone. Conrad remarked:

> Even the purely artistic purpose, that of applying an ironic method to a subject of that kind, was formulated with deliberation and in the earnest belief that ironic treatment alone would enable me to say all I felt I would have to say in scorn as well as in pity.[163]

When presenting villains, Conrad had always been inclined to veer towards caricature, the grotesque and the melodramatic (Donkin in *The Nigger*, Cornelius and Gentleman Brown in *Lord Jim*, for example). The underworld figures of *The Secret Agent* are all boldly and frankly conceived in terms of caricature: Verloc, a paunchy and slothful secret agent; Ossipon, the disciple of Cesare Lombroso's theories who (with his negroid lips, crinkly hair and mongoloid eyes) could serve as an illustration in Lombroso's tomes on criminal anthropology; Yundt, the senile and emaciated terrorist; the grossly corpulent Michaelis; and the puny bomb-making Professor. All these enemies of established society are shown as incapable of (or unwilling to undertake) honest toil; and all except the Professor are parasites on women. But since the narrator maintains such a sardonically ironic stance, the whole work acquires the unity of a macabre and very black comedy. If one expects sober realism, flaws at once dash the expectation: the treatment of anarchism is superficial (there is no glimpse of Kropotkin here), the perpetually bomb-burdened Professor strains belief, and the rapid unmasking of Mr Vladimir by an Assistant Commissioner who strides from his office to the most sordid recesses of Soho and then on to a high-society salon seems to sacrifice all plausibility for the sake of chronological ingenuity. If one reads the tale as satiric savage farce, on the other hand, it offers many satisfactions (even though Conrad's 'scorn' seems then grossly to outweigh his 'pity'): one is the near-Dickensian power of evocation of a London which seems a place of grotesquerie, absurdity, and indomitable dankness and squalor; another is the ferocious gusto in the handling of murder, mayhem and lethal explosion; and another is the sly political irony with which scenes involving the upholders of law and order offer distorted mirror-images of scenes among the conspirators – as when the interview between Heat and the Assistant Commissioner echoes in tone and circumstance the earlier interview between

Verloc and Mr Vladimir. This highly stylised treatment of a conspiracy in a debased urban environment shows Conrad working as a very effective intermediary between the Dickens of *Bleak House* and the Graham Greene of *Brighton Rock*. Conrad was vigorously demonstrating to his readers that he was not to be pigeon-holed as a writer of the sea and of exotic jungles.

In 1948 F. R. Leavis was even to claim that this novel was 'one of Conrad's two supreme masterpieces, one of the two unquestionable classics of the first order that he added to the English novel';[164] but Leavis had been largely anticipated by some of the earliest reviewers. The review in the *Glasgow News* was headed 'A Great Book', and postulated its 'profound and comprehensive knowledge of human nature'; Garnett found further evidence of 'Conrad's superiority over nearly all contemporary English novelists'; and the *Star* declared:

> Since Dickens no novelist has caught the obscure haunting grotesquerie of London. Now Mr. Conrad has caught it, and caught it as wonderfully as he caught the magic of the Malay forest and the magic of the sea.[165]

Other reviewers, however, found it ugly and sordid; *Country Life* even had 'no hesitation in saying that the whole thing is indecent';[166] and these adverse comments remained the dominant ones in Conrad's memory, to judge from the 'Author's Note' which he added to the novel in 1920:

> Some of the admonitions were severe, others had a sorrowful note. . . . . It seems to me now that even an artless person might have foreseen that some criticisms would be based on the ground of sordid surroundings and the moral squalor of the tale. . . . .
> But still I will submit that . . . . . I have not intended to commit a gratuitous outrage on the feelings of mankind.[167]

The importance of the narratorial style to the novel is revealed at once by a reading of the dramatised version. In spite of an early and almost pathological antipathy to actors and acting ('a lot of *wrongheaded* lunatics pretending to be sane'),[168] Conrad's quest for popularity led him to dramatise three of his works. One play was *One Day More*, based on the tale 'To-morrow'; another was *Laugh-*

ing Anne, adapted from 'Because of the Dollars'. *One Day More* had been performed by the Stage Society in 1905, without success; *Laughing Anne* was not performed at all in his lifetime (though a collector paid Conrad £100 for the manuscript). The play of *The Secret Agent* was presented at the Ambassadors' Theatre in November 1922: the acting was proficient but the response from the reviewers was generally hostile; audiences were disappointing and the run ended after just ten performances. As Conrad acknowledged, when the novel is reduced to its 'bare bones' for the stage, 'it makes a grisly skeleton'.[169] Removal of the narratorial voice is indeed a stripping of the flesh; and to fit the chronological and scenic requirements of stage-action the plot has been breathlessly compressed and the locations claustrophobically interiorised. The final moments, in which Ossipon, Inspector Heat, two constables, a detective and the Professor all arrive at Verloc's shop within minutes of the murder, while Winnie relapses into lunacy, could serve almost as a parody of the contrivances of theatrical thrillers.

In 'Heart of Darkness' we are told that to Marlow 'the meaning of an episode was not inside like a kernel but outside, enveloping the tale which brought it out only as a glow brings out a haze'.[170] Comparison of the play-text of *The Secret Agent* with the original novel makes the same point very forcefully. The plot-elements of most Conradian fiction can be found in a wide range of second- and third-rate texts; it is the quality of their authorial scrutiny and descriptive embodiment that generates, in Conrad's narratives, their durable significance.

That significance was slow to gain wide recognition. In England, fewer than 3000 copies of *The Secret Agent* were sold within five years; in the United States the tally was 2500 copies in seven years.[171] Galled by reviewers who treated him as a foreigner (even Garnett referred to him as a 'Slav'), Conrad reflected:

> *The Secret Agent* may be pronounced by now an honourable failure. It brought me neither love nor promise of literary success. I own that I am cast down. I suppose I am a fool to have expected anything else. I suppose there is something in me that is unsympathetic to the general public . . . . . Foreignness I suppose.[172]

In the year of book-publication of *The Secret Agent*, a survey of the twenty-one largest public libraries in Great Britain established that each library held, on average, seven books by Conrad, as against seventeen by Henry James, twenty by Balzac, thirty-nine by Marie Corelli, seventy-seven by Emma Worboise, ninety-one by Mrs Henry Wood and one hundred and nine by M. E. Braddon.[173] To Ada Galsworthy, in January 1909, Conrad remarked disconsolately:

> I have just received the accounts of all my publishers, from which I perceive that all my immortal works (13 in all) have brought me last year something under five pounds in royalties.[174]

4.8 *UNDER WESTERN EYES*

Between December 1907 and January 1910 Conrad completed the manuscript of *Under Western Eyes*, which, like *Lord Jim*, *Nostromo* and *The Secret Agent*, had initially been envisaged as a short story. While working on *Nostromo* he had maintained a flow of payments by dictating the instalments of *The Mirror of the Sea*; and while working on *Under Western Eyes* he dictated instalments of a second autobiographical work, *Some Reminiscences* (eventually re-titled *A Personal Record*): several of these were published in Hueffer's *English Review*, which also was to serialise the new novel.

On completing *Under Western Eyes*, Conrad suffered the worst breakdown of his literary career. His wife reported:

> Poor Conrad is very ill and Dr Hackney says it will be a long time before he is fit for anything requiring mental exertion. . . . . There is the M.S. complete but uncorrected and his fierce refusal to let even I touch it. It lays on a table at the foot of his bed and he lives mixed up in the scenes and holds converse with the characters.
> I have been up with him night and day since Sunday week and he, who is usually so depressed by illness, maintains he is not ill, and accuses the D^r and I of trying to put him into an asylum.[175]

There were several factors which contributed to this breakdown. One was a quarrel with Pinker, who had been advancing

Conrad cheques for £6 per week and had become exasperated by the slow progress of *Under Western Eyes* and by Conrad's recurrent demands for more money. (The author's debts now totalled £2250.)[176] Previously, in July 1909, Conrad had also quarrelled with Hueffer and had declined to submit any more parts of *Some Reminiscences* to the *English Review*. Gout had prevented Conrad from providing an instalment promised for the July number, and Hueffer had criticised the author for discrediting the magazine and for the 'ragged condition' of the material submitted previously.[177] Editorship of the *Review* had magnified Hueffer's tactlessly patronising manner, which Jessie Conrad was not alone in finding insufferable; and soon Conrad was referring to his erstwhile collaborator as 'a megalomaniac who imagines that he is managing the Universe and that everybody treats him with the blackest ingratitude'.[178]

The main factor which precipitated the breakdown was, almost certainly, the imaginative and emotional strain entailed by the writing of à novel which related so directly to the agonies and miseries of Conrad's childhood. *Under Western Eyes* attempts to treat in a cool, impartial manner both the evils of the autocratic regime in Russia and the follies and myopia of the revolutionaries opposed to that regime. Although some of the characters (notably Mme de S—, Peter Ivanovitch and the double agent Nikita) are treated with a satiric vigour reminiscent of *The Secret Agent*, the novel as a whole is written in a more scrupulous and realistic mode; and just as there are careful gradations in the representatives of Tsarism (Prince K— being far more sympathetic than Councillor Mikulin), so, among the revolutionary group, Natalia Haldin and Sophia Antonovna are depicted as genuine idealists in contrast to the charlatan, Peter Ivanovitch. One pessimistic political thesis of the book is that previously expressed in Conrad's essay, 'Autocracy and War': though the repressive autocracy inevitably generates revolutionary conspiracies, a revolution is likely to result only in a new dictatorship. Razumov echoes Conrad's beliefs when he says:

'A violent revolution falls into the hands of narrow-minded fanatics and of tyrannical hypocrites at first. Afterwards comes the turn of all the pretentious intellectual failures of the time. Such are the chiefs and the leaders. You will notice that I have left out the mere rogues. The scrupulous and the just, the noble, humane, and devoted natures; the unselfish and the intelligent may begin a movement – but it passes away from them. They are not the leaders of a revolution. They are its victims: the victims of disgust, of disenchantment – often of remorse. Hopes grotesquely betrayed, ideals caricatured – that is the definition of revolutionary success.'[179]

In formulating such views, Conrad would have in mind the decline of the French Revolution from the era of 'Liberty, Equality, Fraternity' to the time of the Terror and the eventual emergence of Napoleon as dictator–emperor: this would form part of the subject-matter of *The Rover* and *Suspense*. In 1920, three years after the Russian October Revolution, Conrad added to *Under Western Eyes* an 'Author's Note' which declared that he had been vindicated by history:

The ferocity and imbecility of an autocratic rule rejecting all legality and, in fact, basing itself upon complete moral anarchism provokes the no less imbecile and atrocious answer of a purely Utopian revolutionism encompassing destruction by the first means to hand, in the strange conviction that a fundamental change of hearts must follow the downfall of any given human institution. . . . . The oppressors and the oppressed are all Russians together; and the world is brought once more face to face with the truth of the saying that the tiger cannot change his stripes nor the leopard his spots.[180]

Notwithstanding the differences between Poles fighting the Russians for national independence and Russian conspirators seeking the overthrow of Tsarism, the novel's thesis about the corruptibility of revolutionary ideals would inevitably have entailed painful reflections for Conrad about the patriotic idealism of his parents; and the plight of the central character had some connections with Conrad's early situation. Razumov, isolated, lonely, seeking to win a silver medal for an essay and thereby to pursue an academic career, finds himself forced to choose betwen two undesirable political alternatives; and, having betrayed the bomb-throwing Haldin, he steps not into freedom but into new servitude, obliged to serve as a spy the autocratic regime. Conrad had been able to emigrate and, by changing his nationality, to cancel the obligation to serve the Russian state; for Razumov there is only the way of confession, punishment and reclusive retreat. Razumov's watchwords had been: 'History not Theory. Patriotism not Internationalism. Evolution not Revolution. Direction not Destruction. Unity not Disruption.' Zdzisław Najder comments:

> Conrad had every sympathy with the first group of watchwords, but at the same time he saw clearly that within the realm of tsarist Russia these principles were thoroughly pernicious. Thus he had to struggle – to no avail – with his own deeply rooted opinions.[181]

The early, Russian scenes of the book are among the finest in the whole of Conrad's output, and Jocelyn Baines has remarked that 'the characters . . . . . are more subtly and convincingly developed than those in any other of Conrad's novels'.[182] Inevitably, the novel has challenged comparison with Dostoyevsky's work; and, though Conrad regarded Dostoyevsky as 'the grimacing haunted creature' evoking 'fierce mouthings from prehistoric ages',[183] there are some clear links with *Crime and Punishment*. Most obviously, the central character is haunted by memory of his crime and is impelled towards confession; and, in addition, there seem to be various verbal echoes: Razumov's 'Do you conceive the desolation of the thought – no one – to – go – to?' may echo Marmeladov's 'Do you understand . . . . . what it means when you have absolutely nowhere to turn?', while Razumov's 'It was myself, after all, whom I have betrayed' may echo Raskolnikov's 'I murdered myself, not her!'[184] But the relationship between the later novel and the earlier is dialectical rather than derivative. Conrad's greyly pessimistic ending offers dour contrast to Dostoyevsky's vision of love and piety for Raskolnikov, and the (sometimes irritating) use of the teacher of languages as narrator imposes a cool and restrained intermediary voice which contrasts with Dostoyevsky's emotional bounty and impetuous garrulity.

After his breakdown, Conrad revised the manuscript repeatedly. One version was serialised in the *North American Review*, and it contained a large number of stylistic crudities and typographical errors, while retaining passages from the manuscript which later versions omitted.[185] (The book, F. R. Karl states, would be about 30 000 words *shorter* than the serial.)[186] Conrad was more careful in revising the text which appeared in the *English Review*; he hoped that Methuen would set the book from this text, though in the event he was angered by 'the Methuen muddle',[187] which created new variants. The book version published by Harper in the USA is closest to the *English Review* in its first half, but its latter half shares variants with the *North American Review*. Roderick Davis has illustrated the protean nature of the text by specifying in detail, as follows, the variants in one passage. ('D' stands for the text as found in the Collected Edition published by Dent of London in 1947.)

> She turned [over (MS, ER, D) / (omitted in NAR, H)] the pages [greedily (MS, D) / avidly (H, ER) / (omitted in NAR)] for an hour or more, and then [handed (MS, D) / returned (NAR, H, ER)] me the book with a faint sigh. While moving about Russia, she had seen Razumov too. [NAR omits the rest of this paragraph:] He lived[, not (H, ER, D) / (omitted in MS)] "in the centre"[, but "in the south" (H, ER, D) / (omitted in MS)]. She described to me a little two-roomed [wooden (MS, D) / (omitted in H, ER)] house, in the suburb of some very small town, hiding within the high plank fence of a yard overgrown with [nettles (MS, ER, D) / thistles (H)]. He was crippled, ill, getting weaker every day, and Tekla, the Samaritan, tended him unweariedly with [all (H) / (omitted in MS, ER, D)] the [pure (MS, D) / (omitted in H, ER)] joy of [unselfish (MS, D) / natural (H)] devotion. [Nothing could disillusion her in that task. (MS) / There was nothing in that task to become disillusioned about. (H, ER, D)][188]

This brief sample of the many variants does not record differences between the Dent edition and the first Methuen edition or the various intermediate texts published by Doubleday and Heinemann. It nevertheless shows clearly that the circumstances of multiple publication, by providing Conrad with repeated opportunities for revision, have greatly diversified the material available to subsequent editors; and the editorial task is complicated by the knowledge that Conrad's later thoughts are not necessarily superior to the earlier.

When the book appeared in October 1911, it received some very laudatory reviews, and sales in both Britain and the USA were somewhat better than those of *The Secret Agent*. In London,

3000 copies of *Under Western Eyes* were issued; in New York, 4000; and English sales in the two years after publication totalled 4112 copies.[189] Najder estimates that Conrad's income was now about £600 per annum, including the Civil List Pension of £100 a year (awarded in August 1910 'in consideration of his merits as a writer of fiction').[190] Nevertheless, Conrad's saga of debt and renewed borrowing continued; to meet the expenses of operations on Jessie's knee, he was again dependent on John Galsworthy's generosity.

4.9 THE LATER YEARS: *CHANCE* AND ITS AFTERMATH

In February 1914, Conrad's overdraft at the bank was £234, and his debt to Pinker was still vast; but he now stood on the brink of prosperity. The novel *Chance*, published in the previous month in London (after delays caused by a binders' strike) and in New York, was to become, by Conradian standards, a best-seller. More precisely, it was to become a considerable commercial success among readers of the more expensive volumes of fiction (selling at six shillings in Britain and one dollar thirty-five cents in the United States): in Great Britain alone, 13 200 copies would be sold within two years of publication,[191] and American sales were undoubtedly higher. Anyone who reads it today may well have difficulty in seeing why it should have been so decisively successful. *Chance* is certainly not the best of Conrad's novels; nor does the tortuously oblique presentation of the story, with all its ruminations and digressions, seem likely to lend the work popular appeal. Edward Garnett suggested, somewhat cynically, that 'the figure of the lady on the "jacket" . . . . . did more to bring the novel into popular favour than the long review by Sir Sidney Colvin in *The Observer*';[192] but there was nothing exceptional about that jacket. It shows a young, well-clad middle-class lady turning in her chair on deck towards a naval officer who, proffering a shawl, stands protectively over her; it indicates romantic interest but differs little from many such cover-illustrations of the day. Simply the prominence of the woman was probably, for Conrad's sales, the significant image.

A more important factor was that in 1909 Conrad's friend Hugh Clifford had met Gordon Bennett, proprietor of the *New*

York Herald, and had extolled Conrad's writings; so that *Chance* was subsequently serialised in that mass-circulation paper. Another Conrad enthusiast in a key position was Alfred Knopf, who successfully urged his new employer, F. N. Doubleday, to promote vigorously the New York edition of the book. Eventually, Doubleday's firm would produce a sequence of collected editions of the Conrad canon.

The *New York Herald* gave prominent and astute publicity to the serialisation of *Chance* in 1912. First came a series of advance notices; then appeared a striking full-page interview-article on Conrad; and next came the lavishly illustrated serial itself, its opening blazoned across the first inner page of the magazine. Repeatedly the following three selling-points were stressed: first, Conrad is a major writer; secondly, his new novel has been written *especially* for the *New York Herald*; and thirdly, this new work will appeal to *women*. A typical advertisement, for instance, said:

> A sea story that appeals to women is "Chance," by Joseph Conrad, the famous English author. It was written especially for the SUNDAY NEW YORK HERALD, and the first instalment begins next Sunday.[193]

The interview-article was headed: 'Joseph Conrad, Sailor and Author, Writes a New Novel for the New York Herald'; and the sub-heading declared:

> World's Most Famous Author of Sea Stories Has Written "Chance," a Deliciously Characteristic Tale in Which, He Says, He Aimed to Interest Women Particularly. . . . . .

Furthermore, the interview opens with Conrad purportedly telling the paper's representative:

> It gives me the keenest pleasure when I find womankind appreciates my work, and in the story which I am now writing for the NEW YORK HERALD and which begins in the HERALD of January 21 I am treating my subject in a way that will interest women. I don't believe that women have to be written for especially as if they were infants. Women, as far as I have been able to judge, have a grasp of and are interested in the

facts of life. I am not speaking of mere dolls, of course. Such
exist even in a democracy – just as dummy men exist. But any
woman with a heart and mind knows very well that she is an
active partner in the great adventure of humanity on the earth
and feels an interest in all its episodes accordingly.[194]

This is purportedly Conrad's statement when interviewed at his
home; but in fact these opening words transcribe a letter by him
which the *Herald* uses as an illustration on the same page. The
rest of the article describes in detail Conrad's domestic ambiance,
his rural setting in Hamstreet, and his character as an experienced
traveller with an interest in things American. Not only had the
Herald's cheque-book overcome Conrad's customary reluctance
to be interviewed, but also Conrad was clearly lending support
to a selling campaign which held certain ironies. Some of Conrad's
earlier writings (notably *Nostromo* and the letters to Cunninghame
Graham) had expressed hostility to North American materialism
and vulgarity; and his works' emphasis on sea-voyages, colonialism, trade and revolutionary politics had not given the impression
that this author was keen to win the appreciation of women.
Conrad, with the very active encouragement of the *New York
Herald*, was coming to terms with the fact that women and not
men constituted the majority of the fiction-reading public. The
Doubleday edition of the book in 1914 was 'a huge success', and
its associated publicity-campaign entailed promotional stationery
(showing the *Otago* and bearing a quotation from *Chance*), the
formation of a 'Conrad Committee' whose members included
H. L. Mencken and Booth Tarkington, and a scheme to award an
annual Conrad Trophy to 'the most notable piece of American
fiction'.[195]

In England, though reviews of *Chance* were frequently lengthy,
prominent and laudatory, they were not markedly better than
the reviews of *Under Western Eyes*, which had also been well
received; and they certainly expressed reservations about the
intricacies of the narrative method. Indeed, Conrad claimed that
'the *only time* a criticism affected me painfully'[196] was when
Henry James (of all people) complained, in laboured sentences,
that the techniques were needlessly laborious. The pot, with a
vengeance, was calling the kettle black. James said:

> His genius is what is left over from the other, the compromised
> and compromising qualities – the Marlows and their determinant

inventors and interlocutors, the Powells, the Franklins, the Fynes, the tell-tale little dogs, the successive members of a cue from one to the other of which the sense and the interest of the subject have to be passed on together, in the manner of the buckets of water for the improvised extinction of a fire, before reaching our apprehension: all with whatever result, to this apprehension, of a quantity to be allowed for as spilt by the way.[197]

James appears to be magisterially unaware of the irony that his own sentences, so tortuously serpentine, themselves resemble that bucket-chain by which water is passed at the cost of spillage; or indeed that the complaint which he makes of *Chance* ('It places Mr. Conrad absolutely alone as a votary of the way to do a thing that shall make it undergo most doing')[198] might more aptly have been made about the author of *The Ambassadors* and *The Golden Bowl*. James's point was made in blunter form by the reviewer in *Glasgow News*, who, after expressing 'the profoundest admiration and respect for the incontestible genius of Conrad', observed:

> *Chance* suggests a formidable scaffolding that people watch being constructed intricately for days, only to find that in the end it was designed for nothing more than the placing of a weather-cock on a steeple.[199]

In the *Daily Chronicle*, however, David Meldrum loyally affirmed that *Chance* might well be declared the best of Conrad's books; while Sir Sidney Colvin (in the *Observer* article mentioned by Garnett), having deplored Marlow's 'cheap and second-rate' misogyny, felt able to assert:

> *Chance* leaves on the mind the impression of a work of genius in the full sense, and helps to confirm its author's position among the very first of living imaginative writers.[200]

A 'selling' review does not have to be favourable, but it should be *prominent*; and *Chance* was given the place of honour not only in the *Times Literary Supplement* but also in various national daily papers.

Conrad was shrewd when he had told Pinker: 'It's the sort of stuff that *may* have a chance with the public. All of it about a girl and with a steady run of references to women in general all along. . . . . It ought to go down': and he had even re-written the ending to make it 'nicer' – evidently less tragic than in his original conception.[201] The readership of novels was, and still is, predominantly female; and whereas Conrad had previously, on the whole, been dealing with men's actions in masculine situations (colonial adventures, seafaring, political intrigues), now he was offering a novel centred on the embattled psychology of a young woman making her lonely journey to eventual fulfilment in marriage. True, Flora de Barral enjoys only a few years of felicity before her husband, Captain Anthony, is drowned at sea; but, in the final pages, the prospect of a second – and happier – marriage is clearly opened. By Conradian standards, it is an exceptionally positive ending.

The action is confined mainly to south-eastern England and is markedly more domestic in its settings than is customary in Conrad's fiction; and the narrative discusses various public and topical issues. Its depiction of the swindling financier, de Barral, might have brought to mind various well-publicised instances: Jabez Balfour, founder of the Liberator Permanent Benefit Society, who had been jailed in 1895, or Whitaker Wright, of the London and Globe Empire, who had committed suicide after being se.tenced to prison for fraud in 1904. New York had witnessed in 1911 the bankruptcy of Joseph Robin, the morphine-taking financier whose operations resulted in the closing of the Northern Bank and the Washington Savings Bank.[202] Another topical matter on both sides of the Atlantic was, of course, women's suffrage and the feminist upsurge in the years 1905–14. During 1913 the Women's Social and Political Union had gained unprecedented publicity by its campaigns of vandalism and arson (burning churches and other public buildings); on Derby Day, Emily Davison had flung herself to death beneath the hooves of the King's race-horse; and Parliament had passed the notorious 'Cat-and-Mouse Bill', whereby the authorities could discharge feminist hunger-strikers from prison when they became ill and re-imprison them when they had recovered. In Britain, not until 1918 did women (aged thirty and over) gain the right to vote; in the United States full suffrage was attained two years later. Feminism and the associated debates have ample prominence in *Chance*, not only in the satiric presentation of the lesbian Mrs Fyne, whose sexual ideas reflect Sylvia Pankhurst's, but also in the multiplicity of opinions offered by Marlow on the nature and needs of women. Many of these opinions are patronisingly misogynistic, for the radical Marlow of 'Heart of Darkness' has, with the advance of years, become a garrulous reactionary. The plot, too, after its initial satiric treatment of a male-chauvinistic poet, displays a markedly anti-feminist drift: Flora's neurotic insecurity and her inhibitions about marriage have been caused largely by the malevolence of her governess and by the teachings of the 'emancipated' Mrs Fyne; it is to the chivalrous Captain Anthony and the gallant young Powell that she owes her salvation. In view of the hostility offered by many women to the Pankhursts' campaigns, the book's misogyny would not necessarily alienate all its female readers; and certainly it offered them much to think about and argue with. Today Marlow's commentary may repeatedly tempt the reader to scribble angry rejoinders in the margin. He declares, for example:

> As to honour – you know – it's a very fine medieval inheritance which women never got hold of..... In addition they are devoid of decency.....
> The secret scorn of women for the capacity to consider judiciously and to express profoundly a meditated conclusion is unbounded. They have no use for these lofty exercises which they look upon as a sort of purely masculine game..... What women's acuteness really respects are the inept 'ideas' and the sheeplike impulses by which our actions and opinions are determined in matters of real importance. For if women are not rational they are indeed acute..... I am not a feminist.[203]

Over the years, *Chance* has proved to be a divisively problematic novel for its critics. F. R. Leavis, in *The Great Tradition*, ranked it (with some reservations) among the major novels of Conrad. He conceded that Marlow's facile comments may cause some irritation, but proceeded:

> Nevertheless, the view from the outside, the correlated glimpses from different angles, the standing queries and suspended judgements – this treatment, applied by means of Marlow and the complication of witnesses, is, quite plainly, the kind demanded by the essential undertaking of the book. And it is applied

successfully; even the most difficult part of all, the rendering
of the 'tension of the false situation' on board the *Ferndale*,
comes off pretty well (though there is a touch of sentimentality
about the handling of Flora).[204]

And Leavis then gave illustrations of the near-Dickensian descriptive vigour, as when de Barral is observed 'gliding away with
his walk . . . . . as level and wary as his voice. He walked as if he
were carrying a glass full of water on his head.' Leavis concludes
that the combination of descriptive vitality and 'distinction of
mind' makes *Chance* 'certainly a remarkable novel'.

The contrasting, hostile assessment is well represented by
Douglas Hewitt, who sees in *Chance* further evidence of a
decline in Conrad's powers after *The Secret Agent*:

> [I]t seems plain that the later works, in general, show a retreat
> from the degree of awareness of the complexity of emotion
> found in the early ones. The division of mankind into the
> camp of the good and the camp of the bad, for instance, is
> clearly a sign of a restriction rather than a change of interest.[205]

Hewitt remarks that though expectations of irony are aroused by
the titles of the two parts of *Chance* ('The Damsel' and 'The
Knight'), the irony deployed is mild and defensive, for Conrad is
basically endorsing the romantic attitudes and simplifications
indicated by those epitomes of Flora and Anthony. In the case of
Captain Anthony, 'We are required to believe in an unbelievably
fine man. . . . . But we are not convinced of the reality of the
man, nor, therefore, of the significance of the central situation'.
Whereas *Nostromo* or *The Secret Agent* ironically link what seems
good with what seems bad, in *Chance* we are offered a mere
misunderstanding (Anthony's misreading of Flora's inhibitions)
which arises from an excess of virtue. Furthermore, the scene in
which Flora and Anthony at last recognise their mutual love and
desire is burdened with clichés: Anthony's glance is 'full of
unwonted fire', while Flora is 'whiter than the lilies'. Above all,
the oblique techniques of *Chance* are largely specious.

> [I]n *Nostromo*, where shifts in time and viewpoint are also
> common, they enforce criticisms and judgments. But in *Chance*,
> they rarely serve such a function and there is no such sustained

investigation of human motives and actions depending on them.[206]

Hewitt's arguments remain persuasive. In 'Heart of Darkness', the oblique narrative procedures are fully integral with that text's large thematic paradoxes (the eloquent warnings against eloquence, the forceful communication of fears about human incommunication, the complicity of apparent outsiders with the atrocities of colonialism). In *Chance*, the narrative obliquities seem superficial contrivances, often clumsily conspicuous. As Baines noted,[207] the more Marlow explains the availability of witnesses, the more we perceive breaches of the convention at passages where a narrative omniscience is reporting inner experiences or where the purported witness is more the observed than the observer. The garrulous commentary seems to drain and dissipate the symbolic potential of events; and, above all, the conventionally romantic materials of the novel are eventually endorsed instead of being challenged and astringently ironised.

And this feature may, indeed, account for much of the popularity of *Chance*. While its procedures were intricate, the basic emotional spectrum of the novel was reassuringly conventional: the move towards 'normalisation' (i.e. conventionality) in Conrad's outlook preceded his popular acceptance. This is not the whole explanation, of course. Baines says:

> It often happens in the career of a little read but much-praised author that his reputation gradually ripens, book by book, until, like a fruit, it is ready to be sold to the public. This happened with Meredith in the case of *Diana of the Crossways*. . . . . [208]

Year by year, the name of Conrad had been advertised not only by the publishers and the book-reviewers but also by the numerous magazines, on both sides of the Atlantic, which had serialised his work. Conrad had, in addition, completed two long volumes of reminiscential self-publicity, *The Mirror of the Sea* and *Some Reminicences*, which offered an effectively mythologised self. In these books we hear nothing of the neurotic Conrad who would rage at meal-times and flick bread pellets at his guests, nothing of the Conrad who mistakenly threatened his mother-in-law with a shotgun, nothing of the incessant haggling with creditors for further funds; instead, we are offered the image of the author as exiled Pole, experienced seaman, and dedicated writer committed to traditional values of truth, fidelity and honour; one who, by long years of toil, has earned his right to the Olympian survey of humankind from China to Peru. Compared with the largely desk-bound and unadventurous lives of most authors, Conrad offered a romantic, exotic and nobly memorable image; and this was reinforced by the drawings and photographs of himself (neatly bearded, dignified, meditative: a handsome weathered sage) which increasingly accompanied material by and about him in the press. From his anguished complexities he had generated the public self of Conrad as noble seer.

Further support for the notion that a general awareness of Conrad had grown ripe for conversion into a popular readership is lent by the sales-figures for other Conradian works. *'Twixt Land and Sea* (the uneven volume containing 'A Smile of Fortune', 'The Secret Sharer' and 'Freya of the Seven Isles' – two fine tales followed by an abysmal romantic yarn) had emerged quite successfully in 1912: the first English edition numbered 3600 copies, a somewhat larger first printing than for any of Conrad's previous books,[209] and the reviewers' praise was not adulterated by the once-customary warnings about Conrad's gloom or difficulty. Again, in January 1914 *Lord Jim* appeared in a large popular edition: 15 000 copies priced at one shilling, even though Conrad had said 'I would much prefer a new edition at 6/- – leaving the Democracy of the bookstalls to cut its teeth on something softer.'[210] So an early, sophisticated masterpiece had now gained a large public. A further sign of a burgeoning reputation was that in 1912 John Quinn, a collector based in New York, had begun to buy the manuscripts of Conrad's previous publications: £80 for the manuscript of *The Nigger*, £15 for the first draft of 'Youth', and so forth. This proved to be a remarkably astute investment by Quinn, for by 1923 Conrad's success reached such heights that the collector was able to sell the manuscripts at vast profit – Conrad estimated it as 1000%. The manuscript of *Almayer's Folly* then sold for $5300; that of *Chance* for $6600; and even that of a slight tale, 'The Informer', realised $1700.[211]

By 1917 Conrad no longer needed to write for a living: his income in that year was over £2000, and he could renounce his Civil List Pension.[212] The success of *Chance* had enabled Pinker to obtain advances for *Victory* of £1000 for the serial rights (*Munsey's Magazine*) and £850 for the book. For *The Arrow of Gold*, serial rights brought £1200; for *The Rescue* (which Conrad at last finished, twenty-four years after commencement), £3000. Even a short, occasional essay, 'Tradition' (a tribute to British merchant seamen in time of war), was deemed by Lord Northcliffe to be worth £250 for publication in his *Daily Mail* in 1918.[213] (Seventeen years previously Northcliffe had been depicted in *The Inheritors* as Fox, one of the sinister infiltrators of British society.) By 1919, Conrad was amply wealthy, and his vast debts to Pinker and others were cleared; in that year film rights to his work were sold for over £3000.[214] On both sides of the Atlantic plans were afoot for collected editions of his works, to be published by Doubleday in the United States and by Heinemann (later Dent) in Britain. Everything touched by Conrad seemed to be turning to gold, and critical acclaim was swelling to a crescendo – from now on, reviewers' reservations or misgivings were usually expressed within a context which acknowledged his supremacy among fiction-writers in English.

Respect for Conrad was never greater than in the years of his declining powers. That decline, which had been portended as long ago as the depiction of the love-relationship between Lord Jim and his Jewel, was gradual and uneven; to the last he was capable of passages of fine eloquence and memorable beauty. Today most critics would agree, however, that the volume *Within the Tides*, which appeared in February 1915, contained some of his weakest tales: 'The Planter of Malata', 'The Partner', 'The Inn of the Two Witches' and 'Because of the Dollars'. The thesis that Conrad's surge of success was largely powered by his accumulated reputation is supported by the fact that even this collection was generally very well received – and the author himself commented caustically on the verdict of the market-place: '"The Planter of Malata" alone earned eight times as much as "Youth", six times as much as "Heart of Darkness". It makes one sick.'[215] So voracious was Conrad's pessimism that it could even draw nourishment from commercial success.

Victory, which was published later in the same year, further extended Conrad's popularity with the general public, and it still has its critical advocates. Clearly this novel resumes many of the themes that characterised the major fiction: isolation and incommunication; reflection as the foe of practical activity; the

irony that benevolent patronage may do more harm than good;
the paradoxical complicity between the well-meaning person and
his parasitic foe. Thus there are echoes of Decoud in *Nostromo*,
of Lingard in *An Outcast*, of Lord Jim and his encounter with
Gentleman Brown. Yet *Victory* demonstrates that in a work of
literature, the value of a theme depends on its quality of
embodiment. *Victory* begins promisingly with the depiction of
the reclusive Heyst and the web of misunderstanding woven
about him, but the tone falters towards conventionality in the
sexual relationship between Heyst and Lena, and, with the
arrival of the grotesque trio of villains (Jones, Ricardo and
Pedro), Conrad offers melodrama compounded with pretentiously
allegorical rhetoric: Jones is too spectrally satanic, Ricardo too
feline and Pedro too ape-like for belief; and the death of Lena
(who sacrifices her life to prove her love for the man who had
rescued her) is derivative not only from Żeromski but also from
a long line of romantic novels and operas. A reader, noting the
setting and situations (tropical island, seductive heroine living
with gallant rescuer, invasion by three desperadoes, attempted
rape, spectacular conflagration), might almost suspect Conrad of
aiming this work towards Hollywood; and, if that was Conrad's
aim, he hit the target three times, for *Victory* was filmed by
Paramount-Artcraft in 1919, by Paramount in 1930, and again by
Paramount in 1941.[216] The last of these versions re-appeared
recently, on British television: a tritely melodramatic film in
which Hollywood had 'improved' the story by saving Lena and
Heyst from death and conflagration: when the villains are vanquish-
ed, hero and heroine embrace and can live happily ever after.
The exotic, colourful and romantic features in Conrad's writing
have long solicited film-makers, but film versions have tended to
elide the ironies and mordancies of the texts. There is little
doubt, however, that the screening of *An Outcast* in 1952 (director:
Carol Reed; Lingard played by Ralph Richardson) or *Lord Jim* in
1965 (director: Richard Brooks; Peter O'Toole as Jim) helped to
attract a new generation of readers to the novels.

Conrad's emergence into international fame and popular success
coincided with the 1914–18 war, in which his elder son, Borys,
served as an officer in the army, was gassed and suffered shell-
shock. It was to Borys and his comrades that Conrad dedicated
The Shadow-Line (serialised in 1916, book published in 1917), the
novel which is certainly the finest of his last decade. Recollections

of his time as master of the *Otago* always seemed to be peculiarly fruitful in Conrad's imagination: *Otago*-tales included 'Falk', 'A Smile of Fortune' and 'The Secret Sharer'; and *The Shadow-Line* offers a richly evocative account of a purgatorial voyage which is also a moral and psychological ordeal for the young captain. It has its allegorical undertones (those echoes of 'The Ancyent Marinere' and the legend of the Flying Dutchman, and even a hint of a Christ-figure in the artfully-named Ransome), but they reverberate quietly within a predominantly – and convincingly – realistic narrative. And Conrad's style now lacks the conspicuously laboured intensity of *The Nigger of the 'Narcissus'*; it has gained a lucidity and transparency, a lubricated ease of transition from colloquial reflection to lyrical description. More often than not, Conrad's major works are flawed near their endings: one thinks of Marlow's encounter with the Intended in 'Heart of Darkness', or Nostromo's courtship of Giselle; but *The Shadow-Line*, which lacks a sexual theme, is virtually flawless; and readers who endorse this claim will be sympathetic to Thomas Moser's case that, for Conrad, sexual love was a perilous subject which (whether from inhibition or insufficient experience) tempted him towards the conventional and stereotypical.[217] Zdzisław Najder suggests that the preoccupation with sexual love in various novels of the later phase (notably *Chance*, *Victory*, *The Arrow of Gold*) should be regarded not as a cause but as a symptom of Conrad's decline: as he wearied,

> he dealt with women and love more frequently, since the subjects held a promise of broader popularity without requiring greater artistic and intellectual concentration from him; after all, it is easier to be less original and to accept fixed patterns than to create against readers' expectations and contemporary literary fashions.[218]

Hence, one of the saddest impressions given by the novels of Conrad's closing years. Once, he had marched in the vanguard of literary innovation; but now, as a new generation of innovators emerged (T. S. Eliot, Ezra Pound, James Joyce, Virginia Woolf, D. H. Lawrence) Conrad seemed to be retreating from the battle-ground of ideas.

The Arrow of Gold (serialised 1918–20, published as a book in 1919) displays the tell-tale signs of regression towards stereotype, with its adventurous young hero, its psychically wounded but voluptuously beautiful heroine, its grotesquely melodramatic villain, and the rapturous idyll 'in a small house . . . . . embowered with roses'. Conrad had produced the text quite rapidly, largely by dictation, and remarked of the work:

> No colour, no relief, no tonality, the thinnest possible squeaky bubble. And when I've finished with it, I shall go out and sell it in a market place for twenty times the money I had for the *Nigger*. . . . .[219]

Baines suggests that Conrad worked so rapidly that he used the first words that came to mind, instead of seeking the *mot juste*, and readily lapsed into over-writing and melodrama, adding to the typescript many of the 'heightening' adjectives and rhetorical sentences.[220] The early reviewers of the book, while endorsing Conrad's eminent reputation, sometimes indicated disappointment: 'Here and there in its telling the power of the magician wanes', said John Masefield in the *Times Literary Supplement*; and the guarded praise in *New Republic* held a warning:

> *The Arrow of Gold* is one of Mr. Conrad's few open-faced novels. . . . . Seldom has his profound knowledge of human nature seemed so little disquieting.[221]

'So little disquieting', indeed. This 'normalisation' of Conrad's outlook (a regression towards conventionality in the situations, modes and values of the fiction) had various explanations. One was simply the weariness of age; another was his acceptance as an eminent figure. It can be seen partly as cause and partly as consequence of his popularity. Knowledge of the appalling sufferings and losses of the Great War strengthened Conrad's tendency to endorse the traditional values of solidarity and stoical heroism, and curbed his tendency to submit those values to the imaginative tests of a corrosive scepticism.

The Rescue, which Conrad had begun in 1896, was published as a serial in *Land and Water* (London) between January and July 1919, and in *Romance* magazine (New York) between November 1919 and May 1920; the book appeared in May 1920 in the United States and a month later in Great Britain. Conrad had told Garnett:

I am settling my affairs in the world and I should not have liked to leave behind me this evidence of having bitten off more than I could chew. A very vulgar vanity.[222]

Of this novel, however, it could be said, as it has sometimes been said of Henry James's later fiction, that he had chewed more than he had bitten off. The pace of *The Rescue* is heavy and slow, the style is of majestic prolixity; and it develops on a vast scale a sexual thesis that Conrad had more concisely offered in *Almayer's Folly*: the thesis that sexual passion may incapacitate or 'unman' the man of action, so that he becomes spellbound and betrays his allies. It is as though the weariness of Conrad the writer has infiltrated the muscles of his young hero, Lingard; and the exotic setting, the Java Sea and the jungled shore, becomes an opulently coloured dream.

The Rescue is now widely regarded as one of Conrad's most tedious and disappointing novels; to the contemporary reviewers it was further evidence of Conrad's mastery. 'The Rescue is a thing so massive, so profound, so beautiful, so masterly', said the *Sketch*; 'probably the greatest novel of the year', remarked *Punch*; and the *Nation's* long and tactfully-qualified review deemed the novel 'an amazing study of atmosphere, spiritual and physical'. Virginia Woolf, in the *Times Literary Supplement*, made clear her admiration for Conrad ('If he were not Mr. Conrad we should sink all cavil in wonder at the bounty of his gifts'), but proceeded to define her 'cavil', which was that the novel failed in its tragic effect, perhaps because 'Mr. Conrad has attempted a romantic theme and in the middle his belief in romance has failed him'.[223]

The Rover, the last of Conrad's novels to be completed (for he did not live to finish *Suspense*), was serialised in *Pictorial Review* between September and December 1923 and published as a book in December of that year. This Mediterranean novel of the Napoleonic era is much less cumbrous, more economical and lucid, than *The Rescue*, and it gains retrospective poignancy from the partial analogies between Conrad himself and the central character, old Peyrol, who, after many years at sea, retires with his fortune to a farmhouse in the South of France, but then chooses to sacrifice his life in a final display of seamanship for a patriotic cause. Of the predominantly enthusiastic response to *The Rover*, Norman Sherry has remarked: 'The critics might well be gushing, but not for reasons that would satisfy Conrad.'[224]

The Times, for example, declared that 'everyone will read [*The Rover*] with an enjoyment unmitigated by any necessity for intellectual strivings', while the *Spectator* remarked that it belonged to the category represented by G. A. Henty's historical fiction or Stevenson's *Treasure Island* – that of the 'adventure novel beloved of boys'. The *New York Times Book Review* frankly noted the novel's 'commercial' veneer. In Britain alone, the first printing numbered 40 000 copies.[225]

Meanwhile, Conrad's income remained huge. The collected edition of his works brought him £5500; royalties from the recent novels were lucrative; a volume of prefaces or 'Author's Notes' brought £380; and Conrad was continuing to sell his manuscripts – the collector and bibliographer, T. J. Wise, paid £150 for the play-script of *The Secret Agent*.[226] Conrad's inveterate talent for spending more than he earned was sorely challenged by these affluent circumstances but displayed a resilient resistance. In 1919 and 1920 he had managed to spend over £8000,[227] and even in the few remaining years there were times when Conrad occasionally had to borrow (or to undertake public readings in the USA) to meet unexpected financial needs. His son Borys, who had clandestinely married and who was remarkably unfortunate in his quest for steady employment, often needed help: Conrad had given him £1000 as capital, a regular allowance and emergency funds to meet debts. Then there were payments for the education of the younger son, John; Jessie's allowance; the pension for Jessie's mother (Conrad gave her £12–10*s*. per month); and sums rising from £120 to £200 per year were sent to Karola Zagórska, a Polish relative. In 1919 the family had moved into Oswalds, a large Georgian house near Canterbury: its rent and gardening expenses totalled £500 per year; related costs and the running of a car entailed a further £400. Najder estimates that by 1923 Conrad's expenses amounted to the enormous sum of £3500 per year, including the salaries of a secretary and of Jessie's nurse.[228] (The author, who had narrowly evaded bankruptcy in 1904, now contemplated a 'tax exile' in France.) However, the international acclaim and popularity ensured that at Conrad's death, his estate would still be worth over £20 000.[229]

Conrad had hoped in vain for a Nobel Prize, but he declined other honours: among them, the honorary degrees offered him by the Universities of Cambridge, Durham, Edinburgh, Liverpool and Yale, and the knighthood offered in 1924 by Britain's first

Labour premier, Ramsay Macdonald. When the sculptor Epstein visited Oswalds to make his bust of the renowned author, he found Conrad 'crippled with rheumatism, crotchety, nervous, and ill. He said to me, "I am finished".' In July 1924 Conrad suffered a heart attack: 'I begin to feel like a cornered rat', he remarked.[230] Another attack followed, on 2 August; and at 8.30 the next morning he fell dead to the floor.

Around the end of Conrad's life there were some significant discordant notes amid the general crescendo of praise. E. M. Forster, reviewing *Notes on Life and Letters* (1921) complained that 'the secret casket of his genius contains a vapour rather than a jewel'. Leonard Woolf made much the same point (and echoed 'Heart of Darkness') when he remarked of *Suspense* (1925): 'I had the feeling which one gets on cracking a fine, shining, new walnut . . . . . only to find that it has nothing inside it. Most of the later Conrads give one that feeling.' And the *Spectator* said in the same year: 'We begin to see that he was an impressive rather than a likeable writer. . . . . He had stories to tell. And oddly enough he had nothing to say.'[231] Although such sceptical notes were sounded, Conrad's prestige generally remained high with critics and commentators during the 1920s, and, by means of the cinema, with its films of *Victory* (1920), *Lord Jim* (1925), *Nostromo* (1926), *Romance* (1927) and *The Rescue* (1929), his fame was reaching a larger audience than he could have imagined possible when he embarked on his literary career. In the 1930s, as later generations of writers (Lawrence, Joyce, Huxley and Auden among them) moved into the foreground of discussion, there was a slackening of interest in him; the novelist Elizabeth Bowen remarked: 'Conrad is in abeyance. We are not clear yet how to rank him; there is an uncertain pause.'[232]

If any single publication marked the end of that 'uncertain pause', it was F. R. Leavis's *The Great Tradition*, which in 1948 ranked Conrad 'among the very greatest novelists in the language – or any language'; and thereafter the great and still-continuing surge of critical interest swelled, with many of the subsequent commentaries taking as their starting-point the bold discriminations made in Leavis's account. Of course, the vast post-war expansion of higher education in many lands meant that the majority of interesting literary figures soon became, inevitably, the centres of expanding industries of research and commentary; publishers found reliable profits in texts geared to examination requirements. But in the case of Conrad, the scale of the renewed attention has been particularly striking. In addition to numerous critical and biographical studies, several lengthy bibliographies have appeared; computers have produced concordances to most of his works; Cambridge University Press has inaugurated a massively scholarly edition of the entire canon; and Conrad is now served by the international Joseph Conrad Society (which has branches in the USA, the United Kingdom, France, Italy and Poland) and a diversity of periodicals, ranging from *Conradiana*, published thrice-yearly in Texas, to *The Conradian*, published in London, and *L'Epoque Conradienne* (Limoges). There have been post-war adaptations for cinema or television of *An Outcast of the Islands*, 'The Secret Sharer', *Lord Jim*, 'The Duel', *Victory*, *The Secret Agent*, *The Shadow-Line* and *Nostromo*; while Coppola's *Apocalypse Now* (1979) showed how readily 'Heart of Darkness' could be related to the Vietnam War. In addition, *Victory* and the tale 'To-morrow' have been transformed into operas by Richard Rodney Bennett and Tadeusz Baird respectively.

Conrad's range and thematic richness are proven by the diversity of subsequent writers who have testified to his influence: Hemingway, Scott Fitzgerald, Faulkner, André Gide, Thomas Mann, T. S. Eliot, Graham Greene, John le Carré and V. S. Naipaul among them. One of the most distinguished African novels of the 1960s, Ngugi wa Thiong'o's *A Grain of Wheat*, is clearly an adaptation to Kenyan locations of the main themes and situations of *Under Western Eyes*. In short, Conrad's cultural influence has become so extensive and protean that innumerable people, even many who have never read his works, will have had their lives touched and in various ways modified by his. There are ample signs that his major texts have the capacity to infiltrate the cultural era of the computer, the word-processor and the video screen.

In their time, 'An Outpost of Progress', 'Heart of Darkness' and *Nostromo* might have seemed bleakly pessimistic and even cynical about imperialism and international politics; now, they seem far-sightedly realistic. It is not the 'affirmative' Conrad of the later novels but the earlier, acutely sceptical Conrad who now appears the more impressive. Yet that scepticism was never facile, for, explicitly or by implication, Conrad maintained tenaciously the values of honour, courage and humane responsibility; fidelity to humanity and the care for words.

5

Conclusion

The circumstances of Conrad's literary production can be seen as variously enabling, extending, diversifying, inflecting and degrading his creativity.

They were enabling, in the obvious sense that if there had been no commercial market for fiction, Conrad could not have left the merchant marine for a literary career. They extended his creativity by providing a diversity of modes within which he could seek an effective compromise between his imaginative preoccupations and the prospect of financial security: he was impelled to experiment in different literary genres. Further diversification was induced by the complex process of transmission and adaptation of texts, given that both Conrad and local editors might adapt a work for serialisation or modify it for book publication. His circumstances inflected his creativity, for he constantly bore in mind the responses of the immediate British readership; and some of the discrepancies between actual events in his life and their fictional rendition reflect a readiness to flatter British traditions, and particularly the naval traditions. The 'degrading' of his creativity can be seen not only in trivial fiction for the market (tales like 'The Inn of the Two Witches', 'The Brute' or 'Gaspar Ruiz') or occasional essays ('The Heroic Age', 'Christmas Day at Sea') and book-reviewing undertaken simply for the generous payment, but also in the collaboration-works with Hueffer for which the primary motivation was the rapid production of vendible copy. Finally, his circumstances were projectile, in the sense that Garnett, Meldrum, Blackwood and others were consciously helping to project Conrad's works towards an appreciative posterity.

When Edward Garnett's play *The Breaking Point* was banned by the Lord Chamberlain, Conrad supported his friend by writing a sardonic denunciation of censorship, the essay entitled 'The Censor of Plays'; in the event, some of its most scornfully satiric remarks were censored by Garnett. Part 4 of this book has been concerned, in part, with the possibility of the overt or covert censorship of Conrad's works, and with the kinds of pressure that might have been exerted by editors and publishers. The findings seem predominantly reassuring. Among his near-contemporaries, Hardy, Shaw, D. H. Lawrence and James Joyce produced works which were banned or suppressed – in every case, because they were sexually outspoken. Conrad's outspokenness concerned the areas not of sexuality but of epistemology, ontology and politics, where (for his artistic purposes) sufficient tolerance prevailed. Conrad's early novels had little difficulty in gaining acceptance for publication, and the readers and publishers concerned varied from Garnett himself (socialist and even anarchistic in sympathies) and Fisher Unwin (a Liberal) to Henley (the Tory-jingoist friend of Kipling) and Blackwood (Conservative). The texts of Conrad which are most radical and most congenial to left-wing readers are 'Heart of Darkness' and *Nostromo*, both of which comment bitterly on colonialism and economic imperialism; and of these, as we have seen, 'Heart of Darkness' appeared in a Conservative magazine, while *Nostromo* was serialised in a periodical edited by a Liberal Irish Nationalist. There appears no evidence that any publisher or editor attempted to make Conrad change the political or philosophical content of a work. When Heinemann asked the author to change the text of *The Nigger of the 'Narcissus'*, the changes requested were merely deletions of some swearwords; Conrad removed a 'bloody' or two, but not all; and that sufficed. On only one occasion is there clear evidence that Conrad strongly inflected the ideological content of a work so as to harmonise it with the known outlook of an editor, and that was when, aiming at Henley's *New Review*, he was completing *The Nigger*. That inflection may have ensured Henley's acceptance, but, in view of the range of authors published in the *New Review* (a range so wide as to embrace Henry James, Stephen Crane and Arthur Morrison), even this supposition is doubtful; it seems more likely that Henley simply enjoyed the vigour and gusto of the work. Some magazine-editors certainly practised surgery or even butchery on the novels, but an inspection of the text of *Nostromo* in *T.P.'s Weekly* or *The Secret Agent* in *Ridgway's* makes evident that the intention was to divide and arrange the material in conveniently readable instalments: their concern was 'readability' rather than ideological adulteration; and Conrad acquiesced in the procedures, knowing that the book versions would transmit to posterity fuller and more thoroughly meditated texts. Of course, editorial exigencies have their effects on the substance. The serial text of *The Secret Agent*, as we noted, is more like a familiar thriller and less resonant in political ironies than the book; but it is appropriate enough for the relatively casual, entertainment-seeking readership of a popular magazine. Indeed, the inevitable 'institutionalising' of Conrad as a profound author to be interpreted in lecture-halls and seminars, to be earnestly analysed, psycho-analysed and 'deconstructed', may sometimes obscure remembrance that he was, and still is, read by people seeking worthwhile enjoyment who may not be greatly troubled by the battles of evaluation fought in the pages of learned journals. When we see a novel, tale or essay by Conrad situated not in a collected edition on the library shelves but in the pages of a variegated magazine, cheek by jowl with advertisements for whiskey, tobacco and toothpaste, we may gain a healthy sense of the Conrad who, among other things, was an entertainer competing with entertainers – a communicator busily exploiting the first great era of mass communications. The commercial world that he incisively criticised gave Conrad his living and his opportunities for self-expression.

If there was little that could fairly be termed censorship, there was much external and internal pressure on Conrad to compromise with relatively conventional expectations and to blunt the sharp edge of his originality. It is clear, even from the brief selection of reviews quoted in this volume, that a high proportion of reviewers wanted 'a rattling good yarn', a story with a clear, strong, exciting plot; frequently they were baffled by the searching obliquities and the subtle thematics of Conrad's structures. Conrad aspired to a high reputation with the more discerning; but he also needed popularity for financial reasons, and intermittently valued popularity for *ethical* reasons: was he not an avowed spokesman for 'solidarity' and for 'a few very simple ideas; so simple that they must be as old as the hills'? One solution to the problem was a rather cynical expediency: to maintain the flow of payments he would rapidly produce 'bosh' like much of *The Mirror of the Sea* or the more trivial tales, thus gaining time to wrestle with the ambitiously innovative texts. The collaboration with Hueffer was obviously an expedient measure: though their joint ventures were not particularly successful, they were clearly planned as commercial projects. (The reviewers who persistently linked Conrad to

Stevenson may unintentionally have inflicted considerable damage on his literary development.) Some Conradian tales are pot-boilers; some Conradian volumes are collections of mainly ephemeral items. The remarkable range of Conrad's fiction, spanning past and present, maritime and urban, intercontinental and domestic areas, can be seen as, in part, a consequence of his search for a fair compromise between imaginative ambition and general acceptance. The most insidious pressure may have been the internalised pressure to endorse common assumptions by confirming those stereotypes and moral contrasts which the early and major fiction had striven to question and complicate; as he aged and tired, this confirmatory tendency gradually prevailed.

'Judge every man after his deserts, and who shall scape whipping?', asks Hamlet. Conrad once remarked that his admiration for *Bleak House* was so great that he had come to love even its faults: he would not wish them otherwise.[1] The circumstances of his birth, heredity, political situation and temperament entailed on Conrad a life more ravaged by loss and isolation, more embattled and anguished, than most of us experience. His legacy to us is a body of work rich in articulate intelligence, beauty and sensitivity. The final words of this conclusion should simply be an expression of gratitude to Conrad and to the many people who, like Bobrowski (and his tenants) or Blackwood (and his subscribers), helped him to amass for us that legacy.

6

Caudal

6.1 APPENDIX: THE POWER OF THE PROPRIETOR

A sign that the late nineteenth and early twentieth centuries were a halcyon time for publishers is that Conrad was repeatedly in direct contact with proprietors whose firms bore either their own names or the names of their families (and most of those firms survive today, though sometimes in merged and less dynastic forms). When Conrad dealt with the Fisher Unwin firm, he met and corresponded with Fisher Unwin himself, and when he dealt with Blackwood's, he met and corresponded with William Blackwood; similarly, he exchanged letters with Algernon Methuen, who had founded his own publishing house in 1888. Although the intervention of Pinker as literary agent often made Conrad's negotiations more oblique, to the end of his life Conrad was able to meet on personal terms great proprietors like Alfred Harmsworth (of Harmsworth Press and the *Daily Mail*) and F. N. Doubleday (of Doubleday, Page & Co.). To understand Conrad's establishment and progress in his literary career, it is useful to recall some of the powers of the heads of book-publishing houses.

First, there were suasive or directive powers over authors. By advice, encouragement, or contractual specification of word-length and genre (specifying now a novel and now a group of short stories, perhaps a sea-tale or a 'Mediterranean' work), the proprietor could, to some extent, modify and set the immediate pattern of an author's output. Next, there was considerable power over outlets for the resultant work. The proprietor might also be the owner or part-owner of a magazine (Unwin, *Century*; Blackwood, *Blackwood's*; Heinemann, *New Review*, for example). This magazine could serialise material which would later be published in a book, providing publicity and funds for the author and reducing the unit costs of book-publication for the proprietor (since the original typesetting might be re-used, or at least serve as the basis for proofs, for the eventual book). The reader at a publishing house, who had the task of assessing manuscripts and recommending acceptances, might direct the aesthetic revision of a text, and would often, in addition, be a book-reviewer for a magazine, and thus would be in a position to give treble aid to an author he favoured; and he might influence the award of a literary prize. (In 1898 Garnett extolled in the *Academy* Conrad's early work, including *Tales of Unrest*, and soon afterwards the author was gratified to learn that *Tales of Unrest* had won him a share of the *Academy*'s prize for promising new authors.) The proprietor would use publicity of various kinds to increase sales: directly, through advertising in periodicals; less directly, through publicity-releases to the press; and obliquely, by tacit pressure (for favourable reviews) in periodicals which, even if he did not control them, were largely dependent for their survival on advertisements placed by book publishers. Conrad, of course, was well aware of the power of advertising: in 1906 he urged Pinker to persuade Methuen to place additional advertisements for *The Mirror of the Sea*, adding: 'Yesterday Wells was telling us that Kipps hung in the balance till he tackled McMillans and got from them another £100 worth of advertising.'[1] Another proprietorial power was the distribution of the author's work to remote periodicals via syndicates like the Northern Newspaper Syndicate (UK) or the Bachellor Syndicate (USA).

A novel published initially in Great Britain would normally have additional sales in 'the colonies', in various parts of the British Empire. The British firm might have its own branches overseas (Dent: Toronto) or ties with an indigenous firm (Blackwood dealt with Gage in Canada). Given the size and importance of the market in the United States, reciprocal arrangements were commonly made between publishers on each side of the Atlantic (Unwin and Scribner's, or Heinemann and Dodd, Mead, for instance); though some large firms already straddled the ocean (Putnam, New York and London; Macmillan, London and New York). The proprietor would also hope for profits from Europe, either from translation rights or from European publishers who would reprint a text in English: thus Fisher Unwin's contacts with Baron Tauchnitz in Leipzig resulted in the publication of Conrad's *An Outcast* and *Tales of Unrest* in the Tauchnitz Library.

The previous chapters have briefly suggested some Conradian consequences of the availability of this extensive network of proprietors. For Conrad, a happy outcome was that he might receive several payments for one piece of work and could soon establish an international reputation. For scholars and critics, one daunting consequence (given that Conrad was frequently enabled to revise his works) is that a single Conradian text may have a protean variability. For instance, as we have seen, Conrad's late revisions of *Lord Jim* for the British first edition were too late to be incorporated in the Canadian first edition, with the result that Canadian readers and critics encountered a more grotesque and less plausible Gentleman Brown; unwittingly, they were reading an inferior novel. Similarly, reviewers of the first London edition of *The Nigger of the 'Narcissus'* overheard a distinctly more uncouth Donkin than did the readers of various subsequent editions which incorporate authorial modifications. The Conrad novel that we read today may look set and fixed; in his lifetime, it would have shimmered and palpitated with changes as it moved about the world and through the years.

6.2 NOTES PRECEDED BY LIST OF ABBREVIATIONS

Abbreviations appearing among the notes are as follows:

AB: Andrzej Busza, 'Conrad's Polish Literary Background and Some Illustrations of the Influence of Polish Literature on His Work', in *Antemurale*, vol. X (Roma: Institutum Historicum Polonicum, 1966).

CH: Norman Sherry (ed.), *Conrad: The Critical Heritage* (London and Boston: Routledge & Kegan Paul, 1973).

CLJC: Frederick R. Karl and Laurence Davies (eds), *The Collected Letters of Joseph Conrad* (Cambridge: Cambridge University Press; Vol. I, 1983; Vol. II, 1986; Vol. III, 1988).

CPB: Zdzisław Najder (ed.), *Conrad's Polish Background: Letters to and from Polish Friends* (London: Oxford University Press, 1966).

JB: Jocelyn Baines, *Joseph Conrad: A Critical Biography* (London: Weidenfeld and Nicolson, 1960).

JCC: Zdzisław Najder, *Joseph Conrad: A Chronicle* (Cambridge: Cambridge University Press, 1983).

LBM: William Blackburn (ed.), *Joseph Conrad: Letters to William Blackwood and David S. Meldrum* (Durham, North Carolina: Duke University Press, 1958).

LCG: C. T. Watts (ed.), *Joseph Conrad's Letters to R. B. Cunninghame Graham* (London: Cambridge University Press, 1969).

LFC: Edward Garnett (ed.), *Letters from Conrad 1895 to 1924* (London: Nonesuch, 1927).

LL: G. Jean-Aulory (ed.) *Joseph Conrad: Life & Letters* (London: Heinemann, 1927).

Dates are abbreviated in British and not American style: thus 1.4.1896 stands for 1 April 1896 and not 4 January 1896.

Conradian quotations have deliberately been taken from a diversity of editions.

Part 2 (pp. 1–25)

1. *Lord Jim* (Harmondsworth: Penguin, 1986) p. 201.
2. *CPB*, p. 155.
3. *CPB*, pp. 110–11.
4. *CPB*, p. 201.
5. *JB*, p. 96.
6. For example: *CLJC*, II, p. 90.
7. *CPB*, p. 183. Subsequent details of the family's finances are also drawn from Bobrowski's 'Document' in *CPB*.

8. *CPB*, p. 11.
9. JB, p. 32.
10. *JCC*, p. 44.
11. See, for instance, *LCG*, p. 81.
12. *JCC*, p. 41.
13. *CPB*, pp. 40–1.
14. *CPB*, pp. 177.
15. *CPB*, pp. 177–8.
16. *LCG*, p. 75.
17. *CPB*, p. 88.
18. *Industrial Remuneration Conference* (London: Cassell, 1885) p. 52.
19. B. R. Mitchell and P. Deane, *Abstract of British Historical Statistics* (London: Cambridge University Press, 1962) p. 218.
20. E. Blackmore, *The British Mercantile Marine* (London: Griffin, 1897) pp. 134–5.
21. Ian Watt, *Conrad in the Nineteenth Century* (London: Chatto & Windus, 1980) pp. 18–19.
22. *CPB*, p. 148.
23. *CLJC*, I, p. 153.
24. *CLJC*, I, p. 93. Translation: 'quite simply a sordid abomination when preached by civilized people'.
25. *CLJC*, I, p. 112 (my translation of the original French).
26. R. Williams, *Culture and Society 1780–1950* (Harmondsworth: Penguin, 1961) pp. 178–9.
27. John Gross, *The Rise and Fall of the Man of Letters* (London: Weidenfeld and Nicolson, 1969) p. 199.
28. London Library: Conrad's membership (subscription, £3 per annum) kindly confirmed by the staff. Junior Carlton: *LFC*, p. 119.
29. *JCC*, p. 277.
30. Michael Anesko, *Friction with the Market* (New York and Oxford: Oxford University Press, 1986) p. 175.
31. The *Saturday Review*, for instance, reviewed Conrad's 'An Outpost of Progress' when the tale was serialised in *Cosmopolis*.
32. Many of the differences are clearly Conradian, and in some cases the *Forum* phrasing is superior: thus 'She heard the atrocious news' substitutes the idiomatic 'news' for the Gallic 'intelligence' of 'The pretty maid heard the gruesome intelligence'; but I am less persuaded of the general merits of the *Forum* text than is Emily Dalgarno in *Conradiana*, IX (1977), p. 10. She says: '[I]t is curious that this text was not preferred for use in the Doubleday and later book editions.' ('The Duel' was serialised in *Forum* between July and December 1908.)

Part 3 (pp. 26–49)

1. *LFC*, p. 225.
2. AB, p. 126.
3. *LFC*, pp. 188–9.
4. *JCC*, p. 460.

5. AB, p. 120.
6. AB, pp. 124–5.
7. AB, pp. 126, 127.
8. *Fortnightly Review*, vol. CCCCLXIII (1.7.1905) p. 10.
9. P. W. Blackstock and B. F. Hoselitz, *The Russian Menace in Europe* (London: Allen & Unwin, 1953) p. 108.
10. AB, p. 130.
11. AB, p. 148.
12. AB, p. 148.
13. JB, p. 66.
14. *CPB*, pp. 153–4.
15. *CPB*, p. 149.
16. *Under Western Eyes* (London: Methuen, 1911) p. 258.
17. *CPB*, p. 148.
18. W. B. Yeats, *Mythologies* (London: Macmillan, 1959) p. 331.
19. *CPB*, p. 71.
20. JB, pp. 154–5.
21. AB, pp. 152–6.
22. AB, p. 171.
23. A. Mickiewicz, *Forefather's Eve*, tr. D. P. Radin (London: Eyre & Spottiswoode, n.d.) p. 5.
24. A. Mickiewicz, *Konrad Wallenrod*, tr. M. A. Biggs (London: Trübner, 1882) p. 57.
25. Ibid., p. 81.
26. A. Mickiewicz, *Pan Tadeusz*, tr. G. R. Noyes (London: Dent, 1930) pp. 94–8; *Tales of Hearsay* (London: Fisher Unwin, 1925) pp. 114–17.
27. AB, p. 209. The relationship is discussed in detail by Busza (AB, pp. 209–11).
28. JCC, p. 22.
29. *The History of Polish Literature* (Berkeley: University of California Press, 1983) p. 233.
30. M. Giergielewicz, 'Henryk Synkiewicz's American Resonance', *Antemurale*, vol. X, p. 360.
31. *Blackwood's Magazine*, vol. CXLV, pp. 498–513.
32. *Literary News*, vol. XIV, p. 336.
33. *Outlook* (New York) vol. LXVIII (August 1901), cited by Giergielewicz, op. cit., p. 319.
34. F. R. Karl, *Joseph Conrad: The Three Lives* (New York: Farrar, Straus and Giroux, 1979) p. 749.
35. CLJC, III, p. 76 (original in French).
36. AB, pp. 224–30.
37. JCC, p. 474.
38. AB, pp. 216–23; JCC, pp. 394, 581.
39. AB, p. 216.
40. *Victory* (London: Methuen, 1915) p. 410.
41. LFC, p. 309.
42. Conrad may also have taken hints from Maupassant's *Fort comme le mort* and *Le Lys rouge*. See Paul Kirschner, *Conrad: The Psychologist as Artist* (Edinburgh: Oliver & Boyd, 1968) pp. 193–8; and JCC, pp. 394–5.

43. *LCG*, p. 117.
44. *LL*, II, p. 185.
45. *The Nigger of the 'Narcissus'* (London: Penguin, 1988) p. 50. *Lord Jim* (Harmondsworth: Penguin, 1986) p. 51.
46. *Lord Jim*, p. 54.
47. JB, p. 145.
48. *CLJC*, III, pp. 143, 268.
49. *CLJC*, I, p. 111 (original in French).
50. Ian Watt, *Conrad in the Nineteenth Century* (London: Chatto & Windus, 1980) p. 51.
51. G. Jean-Aubry (ed.), *Joseph Conrad: Lettres françaises* (Paris: Gallimard, 1929) p. 52 (original in French).
52. See Kirschner, op. cit., pp. 193–8, 200–5; JB, pp. 146–8; and Cedric Watts, 'Commentary' to *The Nigger of the 'Narcissus'* (London: Penguin, 1988) pp. 141–2.
53. Guy de Maupassant, *Bel-Ami* (Paris: Garnier, 1959) p. 122; *The Nigger* (1988) p. 4.
54. JB, p. 98.
55. Guy de Maupassant, *Contes et nouvelles*, vol. II (Paris: Gallimard, 1979) p. 137 (my translation).
56. *'Twixt Land and Sea* (London: Dent, 1912) p. 48.
57. Kirschner, op. cit., pp. 227–8.
58. Maupassant, *Contes et nouvelles*, vol. II, p. 135 (my translation).
59. *'Twixt Land and Sea*, p. 88.
60. *Conradiana*, vol. XI (1979) pp. 41–61.
61. Anatole France, *Œuvres Complètes*, vol. VI (Paris: Calmann-Lévy, 1926) p. 383 (my translation).
62. *Nostromo* (London and New York: Harper & Brothers, 1904) p. 423.
63. Edmund Spenser, *Faerie Queene*, Bk. I, canto ix, stanza 28.
64. *The Shadow-Line* (London: Dent, 1950) pp. 28, 3, 25, 62, 73.
65. *The Shadow-Line*, p. 109.
66. *The Shadow-Line*, p. 94; *'Typhoon' and Other Stories* (London: Heinemann, 1903) pp. 257–8.
67. *A Personal Record* (London: Dent, 1946) p. 71.
68. *Chance* (London: Methuen, 1914) p. 148.
69. *A Personal Record*, p. 124.
70. *Notes on Life and Letters* (London: Dent, 1921) p. 204.
71. *Bleak House* (London and Glasgow: Collins, 1953) p. 16; *The Shadow-Line*, p. 27.
72. *'Youth', 'Heart of Darkness', 'The End of the Tether'* (London: Dent, 1946) p. 7.
73. Max Beerbohm, ' "The Feast" by J–s–ph C–nr–d', in *A Christmas Garland* (London: Heinemann, 1912) pp. 123–30.
74. John Galsworthy, *Castles in Spain* (London: Heinemann, 1927) p. 91.
75. Kirschner, op. cit., pp. 272–4.
76. *Victory* (London: Methuen, 1915) pp. 221–2; Arthur Schopenhauer, *Essays and Aphorisms* (Harmondsworth: Penguin, 1970) pp. 47–54.
77. Cedric Watts, *Conrad's 'Heart of Darkness': A Critical and Contextual Discussion* (Milan: Mursia, 1977) pp. 85–92.

78.   Cedric Watts, *A Preface to Conrad* (London and New York: Longman, 1982) pp. 94–5.
79.   A reviewer of *Almayer's Folly*, for instance, remarked: 'Mr. Conrad has, we imagine, studied Zola to some purpose' (*Athenaeum*, 25.5.1895, p. 671); while W. L. Courtney, reviewing *The Nigger*, termed Conrad a 'naturalist' (*Daily Telegraph*, 8.12.97, p. 4). See also: Watt, *Conrad in the Nineteenth Century*, p. 45.
80.   *Typhoon and Other Stories* (London: Heinemann, 1903) p. 245.
81.   *The Secret Agent* (London: Methuen, 1907) p. 374. Compare, for instance, the murder of Séverine by Jacques in Zola's *La Bête humaine*.
82.   *Notes on Life and Letters* (London and Toronto: Dent, 1921) p. 17.

Part 4 (pp. 50–130)

1.   M. E. Reynolds, *Memories of John Galsworthy* (London: Hale, 1936) p. 26.
2.   J. D. Gordan discusses the various stages of the writing: see *Joeeph Conrad: The Making of a Novelist* (Cambridge, Massachusetts: Harvard University Press, 1940) pp. 112–29.
3.   JB, p. 135.
4.   *CLJC*, I, p. 170.
5.   Ugo Mursia, *Scritti Conradiani* (Milano: Mursia, 1983) p. 30.
6.   Ibid., p. 32.
7.   *CLJC*, I, p. 341.
8.   Fisher Unwin regularly placed large advertisements in the *Saturday Review* and the *Athenaeum*.
9.   For example: in the *Athenaeum* for 25 May, Unwin's full-page advertisement for his recent publications gives *Almayer's Folly* prominence under the heading 'A NEW ROMANCER'; while, in the *Saturday Review* for 15 June, Unwin's large (half-page) advertisement again gives special prominence to Conrad's novel by quoting a selection of tributes from reviewers.
10.   *CLJC*, II, p. 26.
11.   *CLJC*, I, p. 199.
12.   *LFC*, p. 295. Cf. p. 293: 'I think that every mark of your pen has been attended to.'
13.   C. G. Heilbrun, *The Garnett Family* (London: Allen & Unwin, 1961) pp. 76–7.
14.   Ibid., p. 77.
15.   Ibid., p. 161.
16.   *CLJC*, II, p. 468.
17.   *CLJC*, III, p. 150.
18.   Heilbrun, *The Garnett Family*, p. 76.
19.   *The Inheritors* (New York: McClure, Philips; London: Heinemann; 1901) pp. 67, 69, 70.
20.   *CLJC*, I, p. 292. In the event, paradoxically, it was *The Nigger* which was dedicated to Garnett.
21.   *LFC*, pp. vi, vii.

22. *CLJC*, I, p. 247.
23. *LFC*, p. xiii.
24. *Daily News*, 25.4.1895, p. 6.
25. See Ian Watt, *Conrad in the Nineteenth Century*, pp. 175–9; Cedric Watts, *The Deceptive Text* (Brighton: Harvester, 1984) pp. 43–6.
26. See Watts, *The Deceptive Text*, Chapters 3 and 5.
27. *CLJC*, I, p. 247.
28. 'Author's Note' to *Almayer's Folly* (London: Heinemann, 1921) p. ix.
29. *World*, 15.5.95, p. 31; *Nation*, 17.10.95, p. 278.
30. *Bookman*, September 1896, p. 176; *Academy*, 15.6.95, p. 52.
31. *Scotsman*, 29.4.95, p. 3; *Daily Chronicle*, 11.5.95, p. 3; *Athenaeum*, 25.5.95, p. 671; *Saturday Review*, 15.6.95, p. 797; *Speaker*, 29.6.95, p. 723.
32. *Literary News*, September 1895, pp. 268–9; *Spectator*, 19.10.95, p. 530.
33. *Weekly Sun*, 9.6.95, pp. 1–2.
34. *CLJC*, I, p. 219.
35. *CLJC*, I, p. 214.
36. *LFC*, pp. xx–xxi. Though Garnett said that *Almayer's Folly* took 'seven years' to reach its third impression, the publisher specified *nineteen* years: see *Almayer's Folly* (London: Fisher Unwin, 1925) p. 4.
37. *CLJC*, I, p. 266.
38. *Glasgow Herald*, 19.3.96, p. 10.
39. *Manchester Guardian*, 19.5.96, p. 5.
40. *Saturday Review*, 10.5.96, pp. 509–10.
41. *Boon* (London: Unwin, 1915) pp. 144–5; cf. *Experiment in Autobiography*, vol. II (London: Gollancz, 1934) pp. 615–23.
42. *JCC*, p. 199.
43. *CLJC*, I, pp. 240, 306. Unwin's usual royalty terms were 10% on the first 2000 copies, 12½% on the second 2000, and 15% thereafter. Conrad eventually, in his late days of success, would gain royalties as high as 25%.
44. Thomas Moser, *Joseph Conrad: Achievement and Decline* (Cambridge, Massachusetts: Harvard University Press, 1957) Chap. II.
45. 'Author's Note' to *Tales of Unrest* (London: Dent, 1947) p. viii.
46. *Literature* (London), 30.4.98, p. 508. Conrad's 'realism' was contrasted unfavourably with Henry Harland's 'romance'.
47. *LFC*, p. xxvi.
48. *CLJC*, I, pp. 285, 301.
49. *CLJC*, I, p. 350. *Cosmopolis*, which lasted only from 1896 to 1898, was published in London by Unwin and in New York by the International News Company.
50. *CLJC*, I, p. 293.
51. *CLJC*, I, p. 366; *LBM*, pp. 3–4.
52. A. L. Bowley, *Wages and Income in the United Kingdom since 1860* (London: Cambridge University Press, 1937) p. 49.
53. N. Sherry, *Conrad's Western World* (London: Cambridge University Press, 1971) pp. 330–2; *CLJC*, I, p. 350.

54. *CLJC*, I, pp. 319, 386.
55. *CLJC*, I, pp. 308–9.
56. *CLJC*, I, p. 329.
57. *CLJC*, I, p. 319.
58. *The Nigger of the 'Narcissus'* (London: Penguin, 1988), p. xlvi.
59. *CLJC*, I, p. 323; III, p. 115.
60. *Last Essays* (London: Dent, 1955) p. 95.
61. *CLJC*, I, p. 416; II, pp. 4, 242; *Last Essays* (London: Dent, 1955) pp. 102–3, 120–1, 123–4.
62. *CLJC*, I, p. 398.
63. 'Echoes: IV' in *Poems* (London: Nutt, 1898) p. 119. The poem is dated 1875.
64. *New Review*, vol. XVII (September 1897) pp. 317, 319.
65. Henley's comment on socialism is quoted in John Connell's *W. E. Henley* (London: Constable, 1949) p. 153.
66. Rudyard Kipling, *Something of Myself* (Harmondsworth: Penguin, 1987) p. 82.
67. 'Rhymes and Rhythms XXV' in *Poems*, pp. 254–5.
68. *New Review*, vol. XVII (September 1897) pp. 241–2; *The Nigger of the 'Narcissus'* (London: Heinemann, 1897) pp. 58–9. (Identical passages.)
69. *CLJC*, I, p. 211.
70. Henley collaborated with John S. Farmer to produce a seven-volume dictionary, *Slang and its Analogues*, which had entries for 'cunt', 'tool', etc.; the entry for 'bloody' cited Dana's *Two Years before the Mast* – an autobiography which influenced *The Nigger*.
71. *Daily Telegraph*, 8.12.1897, p. 4.
72. *CLJC*, I, p. 395. (Heinemann was *not* an 'Israelite'.)
73. 'Slaves of the Lamp' appeared in the issues for April and May 1897; years later, Kipling wrote to Conrad to praise *The Mirror of the Sea*.
74. *CLJC*, I, p. 320.
75. *CLJC*, I, p. 372.
76. *New Review*, vol. XVII (December 1897) p. 621; *The Nigger of the 'Narcissus'* (London: Heinemann, 1897) p. 243.
77. *New Review*, vol. XVII (December 1897) p. 623; *The Nigger* (London: Heinemann, 1897) p. 249.
78. *Daily Mail*, 7.12.97, p. 3; *Daily Telegraph*, 8.12.97, p. 4; *Saturday Review*, 29.1.98, pp. 145–6, and 12.2.98, p. 211.
79. *Glasgow Herald*, 9.12.97, p. 10; *Spectator*, 25.12.97, p. 940; *Star*, 16.12.97, p. 1.
80. *CLJC*, I, p. 429; II, pp. 19–20; I, pp. 409–10.
81. *Blackwood's Magazine*, vol. CLXIV (September 1898) p. 323.
82. Jerry Allen, *The Sea Years of Joseph Conrad* (London: Methuen, 1967) p. 319; she specifies the crew at the time of the shipwreck.
83. *LBM*, p. xv; *CLJC*, II, p. 418.
84. *LBM*, pp. 123–4, 149; 120, 121, 144, 197.
85. *CLJC*, II, p. 328.
86. *LBM*, pp. 20–21.

87. *LBM*, p. 40.
88. *LBM*, p. 97, 99–100, 101.
89. *LBM*, p. 86.
90. *LBM*, p. 184.
91. JB, p. 281.
92. *CLJC*, II, pp. 416, 418.
93. JB, pp. 284–5.
94. *CLJC*, II, p. 162.
95. *Daily Chronicle*, 22.12.97, p. 3; *Academy*, 1.1.98, pp. 1–2.
96. *Blackwood's Magazine*, vol. CLXV (March 1899) p. 619.
97. *CLJC*, II, pp. 139–40.
98. *Blackwood's Magazine*, vol. CLXV (February 1899) p. 196.
99. *LBM*, p. 49.
100. *Academy and Literature*, 6.12.02, p. 606; *Manchester Guardian*, 10.12.02, p. 3.
101. *LBM*, p. 199.
102. *CLJC*, II, p. 417.
103. *LBM*, pp. 91–2.
104. *Manchester Guardian*, 29.10.1900, p. 6; *Speaker*, 24.11.1900, pp. 215–16; *Daily Telegraph*, 7.11.1900, p. 11; *Sketch*, 14.11.1900, p. 142.
105. *LBM*, p. 199.
106. See Ernest W. Sullivan, *The Several Endings of Joseph Conrad's Lord Jim* (London: Joseph Conrad Society, n.d.).
107. F. M. Ford, *Joseph Conrad: A Personal Remembrance* (London: Duckworth, 1924) p. 52.
108. James Hepburn, *The Author's Empty Purse* (London: Oxford University Press, 1968) p. 42.
109. Ibid., p. 1.
110. Michael Anesko, *Friction with the Market* (New York and Oxford: Oxford University Press, 1986) p. 142.
111. Ibid., p. 172.
112. *CLJC*, II, p. 195.
113. *JCC*, p. 275.
114. *JCC*, p. 276.
115. *JCC*, p. 335.
116. *CLJC*, III, p. 257.
117. *JCC*, pp. 352, 369.
118. *CLJC*, III, p. 405. Pinker had previously supplied a pen: III, p. 317.
119. *JCC*, p. 356.
120. F. M. Ford, *Return to Yesterday* (New York: Liveright, 1972) p. 33; *CLJC*, II, p. 319.
121. JB, p. 427.
122. *LL*, II, p. 266.
123. Hepburn, *The Author's Empty Purse*, p. 96.
124. *CLJC*, II, p. 334.
125. *CLJC*, III, p. 120, 142, 167; *JCC*, p. 298.
126. *CLJC*, III, pp. 24, 28.

127. Arthur Mizener, *The Saddest Story* (New York and Cleveland: World Publishing Company, 1971) pp. 89–91; *JCC*, pp. 299–300.
128. *JCC*, pp. 284–5, 273, 277, 296. 'To-morrow' was ' "Conrad" adapted down to the needs of a magazine' (*CLJC*, II, p. 373).
129. See M. Curreli and C. Watts, 'Conrad and Zangwill', in *Kwartalnik Neofilologiczny* (Warszawa) vol. XXII (1975) pp. 240–2.
130. F. M. Ford, *The Good Soldier* (London: Heinemann, 1970) p. 11.
131. *JCC*, pp. 238–9.
132. *Daily Chronicle*, 11.7.01, p. 3; *Scotsman*, 4.7.01, p. 2; *Manchester Guardian*, 10.7.01, p. 4; *Daily Telegraph*, 14.7.01, p. 9; *Daily News*, 24.7.01, p. 8.
133. *CLJC*, II, p. 257.
134. Ford, *Joseph Conrad: A Personal Remembrance*, p. 134.
135. *CLJC*, II, pp. 296, 409, 414–15.
136. *CLJC*, III, p. 60.
137. *CLJC*, II, p. 357. Two thirds of the final text of *Romance* were by Hueffer.
138. *CLJC*, II, p. 366.
139. *CLJC*, III, p. 74.
140. *CLJC*, III, p. 140.
141. *CLJC*, III, p. 112.
142. *Mirror*: the *Pall Mall Magazine* offered Conrad six guineas per thousand words: *CLJC*, III, p. 142. *Nostromo*: *CLJC*, III, p. 17.
143. *CLJC*, III, p. 142; *JCC*, pp. 298, 555.
144. *The Mirror of the Sea* (London: Methuen, 1906), p. 143.
145. *JB*, pp. 326–7.
146. Holograph inscription in T. J. Wise's copy of *Nostromo* (British Library, Ashley 463).
147. *Sun*, 9.6.95, pp. 1–2.
148. *T.P.'s Weekly*, vol. III (15.1.04) p. 81; vol. III (5.2.04) p. 194. M.K.S.'s praise of Conrad was echoed by 'C.M.' of Wallington: vol. III (18.3.04) p. 390.
149. *CLJC*, III, p. 167.
150. *CLJC*, III, pp. 91–2.
151. *CLJC*, III, p. 92.
152. Beggars: *T.P.'s Weekly*, vol. III (26.2.04) p. 270; hides; vol. III (22.4.04) p. 530. See also: *Nostromo*, ed. Keith Carabine (Oxford: Oxford University Press, 1984) pp. 580, 584.
153. *Nostromo* (London and New York: Harper, 1904) pp. 422–3.
154. Ibid, pp. 442–3.
155. *T.P.'s Weekly*, vol. IV (7.10.04) p. 456.
156. *TLS*, 21.10.04, p. 320; *Daily Telegraph*, 9.11.04, p. 4; *British Weekly*, 10.11.04, p. 129; *Manchester Guardian*, 2.11.04, p. 5.
157. *Speaker*, 12.11.04, p. 138–9; *Illustrated London News*, 26.11.04, p. 774.
158. Emily K. Dalgarno, 'Conrad, Pinker, and the Writing of *The Secret Agent*', in *Conradiana*, vol. IX (1977) p. 51.
159. Ibid., pp. 50, 52.
160. Ibid., pp. 55, 56.
161. *Ridgway's*, 6.10.06, p. 12.

162. 'Author's Note' to *The Secret Agent* (London: Dent, 1947) p. x; see also Norman Sherry, *Conrad's Western World* (London: Cambridge University Press, 1971) Chapter 22.
163. 'Author's Note' to *The Secret Agent*, p. xiii.
164. F. R. Leavis, *The Great Tradition* [1948] (Harmondsworth: Penguin, 1962) p. 242.
165. *Glasgow News*, 3.10.07, p. 5; *Nation*, 28.9.07, p. 1096; *Star*, 5.10.07, p. 1.
166. *Country Life*, 21.9.07, p. 404.
167. 'Author's Note' to *The Secret Agent*, pp. vii, xv.
168. *LCG*, p. 50.
169. 'Author's Note' to *The Secret Agent*, p. xv.
170. *Blackwood's Magazine* (February 1895) p. 195.
171. *JCC*, p. 332.
172. *LL*, II, p. 65.
173. D. Hudson, 'Reading', in S. Nowell-Smith (ed.) *Edwardian England* (London: Oxford University Press, 1964) pp. 310–11.
174. *LL*, II, p. 94. The sum would be the remainder after repayments to Pinker.
175. *LBM*, p. 192.
176. *JCC*, pp. 354–6, 352.
177. *LL*, II, pp. 101–2.
178. *JCC*, p. 351.
179. *Under Western Eyes* (London: Methuen, 1911), p. 132.
180. Ibid., p. xiii.
181. *JCC*, p. 359.
182. *JB*, pp. 361–2.
183. *LFC*, pp. 269, 260.
184. *JB*, p. 370, suggests these and other analogies.
185. Roderick Davis, '*Under Western Eyes*: "The Most Deeply Meditated Novel"', *Conradiana*, vol. IX (1977) p. 72.
186. F. R. Karl, *Joseph Conrad: The Three Lives* (New York: Farrar, Straus and Giroux, 1979) p. 703.
187. Davis, op. cit., p. 73.
188. Ibid., p. 74.
189. *JCC*, pp. 372, 574; *JB*, p. 380. (The figures appear to contradict Najder's claim that the sales were worse than those of *The Secret Agent*.)
190. *JCC*, pp. 369, 366.
191. *JCC*, p. 390; *JB*, p. 380.
192. *LFC*, p. xx.
193. *New York Herald*, 14.1.12, p. 5.
194. *New York Herald*, 14.1.12, Magazine Section, p. 3.
195. William V. Costanzo, 'Conrad's American Visit', *Conradiana*, vol. XIII (1981) p. 11.
196. *JB*, p. 383.
197. 'The New Novel' in *Notes on Novelists* (London: Dent, 1914) p. 278. (This essay is an expansion of 'The Younger Generation', *TLS*, 19.3.14, pp. 133–4, and 2.4.14, pp. 157–8.)

198. *Notes on Novelists*, p. 274.
199. *Glasgow News*, 5.2.14, p. 10.
200. *Daily Chronicle*, 15.1.14, p. 4; *Observer*, 18.1.14, p. 5.
201. JB, pp. 381, 382.
202. Robin: see *New York Herald*, 21.1.11, p. 13.
203. *Chance* (London: Methuen, 1914) pp. 56, 132–3.
204. F. R. Leavis, *The Great Tradition* (Harmondsworth: Penguin, 1962) p. 246.
205. D. Hewitt, *Conrad: A Reassessment* (London: Bowes & Bowes, 1975) p. 89.
206. Ibid., p. 98.
207. JB, p. 383.
208. JB, p. 380.
209. JCC, p. 380.
210. JCC, p. 391.
211. JB, p. 433.
212. JB, p. 404; JCC, p. 425.
213. JCC, p. 429.
214. JCC, p. 442.
215. JCC, p. 407.
216. K. A. Lohf and E. P. Sheehy, *Joseph Conrad at Mid-Century* (Minneapolis: University of Minneapolis Press, 1957) p. 38.
217. Thomas Moser, *Joseph Conrad: Achievement and Decline* (Cambridge, Massachusetts: Harvard University Press, 1957) Chapter II.
218. JCC, p. 363.
219. LL, II, p. 198.
220. JB, p. 411.
221. TLS, 7.8.19, p. 422; *New Republic*, 10.5.19, p. 56.
222. LFC, pp. 287–8.
223. *Sketch*, 21.7.20, p. 428; *Punch*, 14.7.20, p. 39; *Nation*, 17.7.20, pp. 503–4; TLS, 1.7.20, p. 419.
224. CH, p. 35.
225. *Times*, 3.12.23, p. 15; *Spectator*, 15.12.23, pp. 960–1; *New York Times Book Review*, 2.12.23, pp. 6, 22; JCC, p. 485.
226. JCC, p. 453.
227. JCC, p. 453.
228. JCC, p. 479.
229. JCC, p. 608.
230. *Epstein: An Autobiography* (London: Hulton Press, 1955) p. 74; JCC, p. 490.
231. Forster: 'Joseph Conrad: A Note' (dated by Forster '1920', but the date should be 1921) in *Abinger Harvest* (London: Nelson, 1936) p. 135; Woolf: *Nation and Athenaeum*, 3.10.25, p. 18; *Spectator*, 10.10.25, pp. 613–14.
232. CH, p. 39.

Part 5 (pp. 131–4)

1. *A Personal Record* (London: Dent, 1946) p. 124.

Part 6 (Appendix)

1. *CLJC*, III, p. 314. Hueffer recalled that when the advertising campaign for *Romance* ceased, so did sales of the book.

6.3 BIBLIOGRAPHY (IN CHRONOLOGICAL ORDER)

Edward Garnett (ed.), *Letters from Conrad 1895 to 1924* (London: Nonesuch, 1927).

G. Jean-Aubry (ed.), *Joseph Conrad: Life & Letters* (London: Heinemann, 1927).

F. R. Leavis, *The Great Tradition* [1948] (Harmondsworth: Penguin, 1962).

Thomas Moser, *Joseph Conrad: Achievement and Decline* (Cambridge, Massachusetts: Harvard University Press, 1957).

K. A. Lohf and E. P. Sheehy, *Joseph Conrad at Mid-Century* (Minneapolis: University of Minnesota Press, 1957).

W. Blackburn (ed.), *Joseph Conrad: Letters to William Blackwood and David S. Meldrum* (Durham, North Carolina: Duke University Press, 1958).

Jocelyn Baines, *Joseph Conrad: A Critical Biography* (London: Weidenfeld and Nicolson, 1960).

C. G. Heilbrun, *The Garnett Family* (London: Allen & Unwin, 1961).

Andrzej Busza, 'Conrad's Polish Literary Background and Some Illustrations of the Influence of Polish Literature on His Work', in *Antemurale*, vol. X (Roma: Institutum Historicum Polonicum, 1966).

Zdzisław Najder (ed.), *Conrad's Polish Background: Letters to and from Polish Friends* (London: Oxford University Press, 1966).

Conradiana (Lubbock, Texas: 1968 onwards).

Cedric Watts (ed.), *Joseph Conrad's Letters to R. B. Cunninghame Graham* (London: Cambridge University Press, 1969).

T. G. Ehrsam, *A Bibliography of Joseph Conrad* (Metuchen, New Jersey: Scarecrow Press, 1969).

B. E. Teets and H. E. Gerber, *Joseph Conrad: An Annotated Bibliography of Writings about Him* (De Kalb, Illinois: Northern Illinois University Press, 1971).

Norman Sherry (ed.), *Conrad: The Critical Heritage* (London: Routledge & Kegan Paul, 1973).

Douglas Hewitt, *Conrad: A Reassessment* (London: Bowes & Bowes, 1975).

Ian Watt, *Conrad in the Nineteenth Century* (London: Chatto & Windus, 1980).

Cedric Watts, *A Preface to Conrad* (London and New York: Longman, 1982).

Zdzisław Najder, *Joseph Conrad: A Chronicle* (Cambridge: Cambridge University Press, 1983).

Frederick R. Karl and Laurence Davies (eds), *The Collected Letters of Joseph Conrad* (Cambridge: Cambridge University Press; Vol. I, 1983; Vol. II, 1986; Vol. III, 1988).

Cedric Watts, *The Deceptive Text* (Brighton: Harvester, 1984).

6.4 INDEX

Literary works are listed under their authors' names.

Index